CAMBRIDGE LIBRARY COLLECTION

Books of enduring scholarly value

Travel and Exploration

The history of travel writing dates back to the Bible, Caesar, the Vikings and the Crusaders, and its many themes include war, trade, science and recreation. Explorers from Columbus to Cook charted lands not previously visited by Western travellers, and were followed by merchants, missionaries, and colonists, who wrote accounts of their experiences. The development of steam power in the nineteenth century provided opportunities for increasing numbers of 'ordinary' people to travel further, more economically, and more safely, and resulted in great enthusiasm for travel writing among the reading public. Works included in this series range from first-hand descriptions of previously unrecorded places, to literary accounts of the strange habits of foreigners, to examples of the burgeoning numbers of guidebooks produced to satisfy the needs of a new kind of traveller - the tourist.

The Foreigner in Far Cathay

Walter Medhurst's 1872 book traces his personal impressions of nineteenth-century Chinese society. The author is determined to give a picture of the country and its inhabitants that is realistic and free of the tired clichés often found in contemporary Western accounts of the country. Medhurst engages with a wide spectrum of Chinese traditions and habits: looking at the characteristics of advertising and how Chinese newspapers are run; describing opium-smoking and Chinese burial customs; delving into the relationship between men and women; and sampling the delights of Chinese cuisine. He also writes about the position of foreign citizens in China and focuses on the relationship between China and the Western world. Concerned that the West should show China the respect it deserves, he attempts especially to capture the essence of the Chinese character.

T0382124

Cambridge University Press has long been a pioneer in the reissuing of out-of-print titles from its own backlist, producing digital reprints of books that are still sought after by scholars and students but could not be reprinted economically using traditional technology. The Cambridge Library Collection extends this activity to a wider range of books which are still of importance to researchers and professionals, either for the source material they contain, or as landmarks in the history of their academic discipline.

Drawing from the world-renowned collections in the Cambridge University Library, and guided by the advice of experts in each subject area, Cambridge University Press is using state-of-the-art scanning machines in its own Printing House to capture the content of each book selected for inclusion. The files are processed to give a consistently clear, crisp image, and the books finished to the high quality standard for which the Press is recognised around the world. The latest print-on-demand technology ensures that the books will remain available indefinitely, and that orders for single or multiple copies can quickly be supplied.

The Cambridge Library Collection will bring back to life books of enduring scholarly value (including out-of-copyright works originally issued by other publishers) across a wide range of disciplines in the humanities and social sciences and in science and technology.

The Foreigner in Far Cathay

WALTER HENRY MEDHURST

CAMBRIDGE UNIVERSITY PRESS

Cambridge, New York, Melbourne, Madrid, Cape Town, Singapore,
São Paolo, Delhi, Dubai, Tokyo

Published in the United States of America by Cambridge University Press, New York

www.cambridge.org
Information on this title: www.cambridge.org/9781108014687

© in this compilation Cambridge University Press 2010

This edition first published 1872
This digitally printed version 2010

ISBN 978-1-108-01468-7 Paperback

The original edition of this book contains a number of colour plates, which cannot
be printed cost-effectively in the current state of technology. The colour scans
will, however, be incorporated in the online version of this reissue, and in printed
copies when this becomes feasible while maintaining affordable prices.

Additional resources for this publication at www.cambridge.org/9781108014687

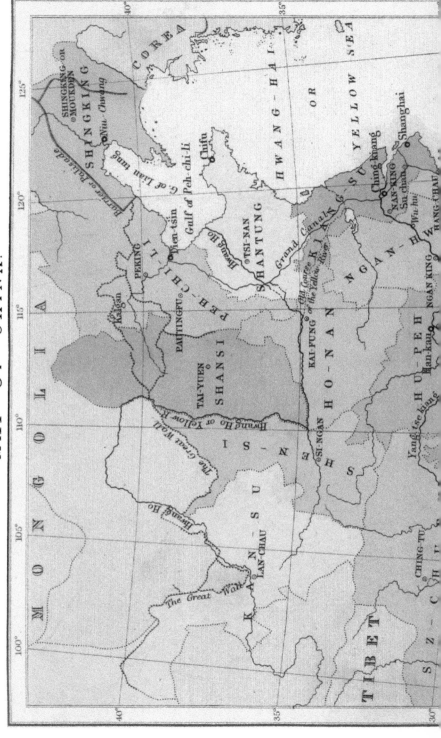

MAP OF CHINA.

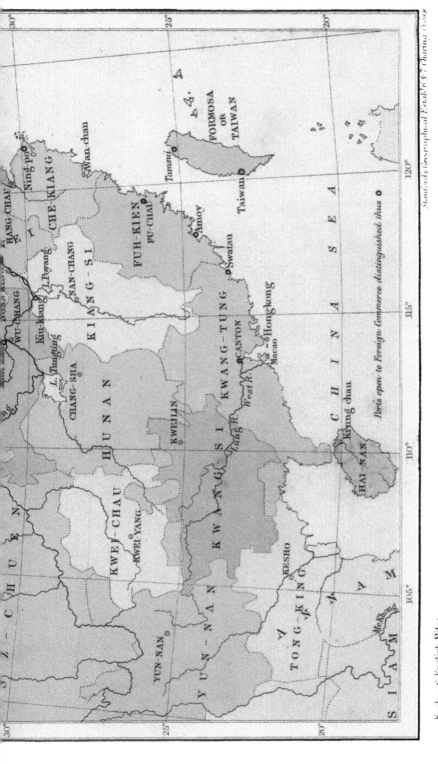

Scale of English Miles

Stanford's Geographical Estab^t 6 & 7 Charing Cross

Ports open to Foreign Commerce distinguished thus ⊙

CHINA SEA

FORMOSA OR TAIWAN

SI-CHUEN
CHE-KIANG
KIANG-SI
FUH-KIEN
HUNAN
KWEI-CHAU
KWANG-SI
KWANG-TUNG
YUN-NAN
HAI-NAN
TONG-KING
SIAM

Ning-poo
HANG-CHAU
Wan-chau
NAN-CHANG
L.Poyang
WU-CHANG
Kiu-kiang
Tungting
L.Tungting
CHANG-SHA
KWEILIN
PU-CHAU
Amoy
Swatau
Tamsui
Taiwan
CANTON
Hongkong
Macao
Kiung chau
KWEI-YANG
YUN-NAN
KESHO
Me.Khong
West R.
Ping R.

THE

FOREIGNER IN FAR CATHAY.

BY

W. H. MEDHURST,

H.B.M. CONSUL, SHANGHAI.

With Map.

LONDON:

EDWARD STANFORD, 6 & 7, CHARING CROSS, S.W.

—

1872.

CONTENTS.

PREFACE.

THIS little book does not pretend to the importance of a work on China. Its aim is simply to enlighten the home public as to the actual circumstances in which residents in that remote region find themselves, and to supply a few scraps of information, part of it new, and part of it hitherto misapprehended, respecting the Chinese themselves. Existing relations between China and the leading Western powers are inevitably tending towards results, the importance of which to both sides cannot be exaggerated, and I shall consider myself fortunate if the few words, which I have herein ventured, should lead to a better understanding in England of our true position and interests in " Far Cathay."

W. H. MEDHURST.

ATHENÆUM CLUB.
August, 1872.

THE

FOREIGNER IN FAR CATHAY.

CHAPTER I.

INTRODUCTORY.

ALTHOUGH numerous bulky volumes have
been written upon China and the Chinese, and
intercommunication with Western countries
has been vastly extended of late years, it is
marvellous how vague, and in some cases how
erroneous, are the popular notions prevalent
in Europe and America in regard to the country and our relations with it. Everyone believes
perhaps, and rightly, that China counts her
population by hundreds of millions, and that
her territory occupies a very considerable proportion of the Asiatic continent; and misty
impressions are cherished no doubt as to the
existence of evidences of an advanced state of
civilization in the way of a literature, a philo-
sophy, a highly-perfected social system, and so

on. But test the information a little further,
and it will be found that the prominent idea
with regard to a Chinaman is that he is a
quaint but stolid besotted creature, who smokes
opium perpetually, and drowns his daughters
as fast as they appear; whose every-day food
consists of puppies, kittens, rats, and such like
garbage; whose notions of honour, honesty,
and courage, are of the loosest; and to whom
cruelty is a pastime. This opinion may not
quite tally with the impressions as to civilization and social advancement above alluded to,
but no trouble is taken to explain the contra-
diction, and the more ridiculous andfamiliar
fancy is indulged in.

Even less perhaps is known respecting the
communities of our countrymen and other
foreigners who make China a place of resort
either for their own profit or for the benefit of
the natives. If speculations on the subject
take any shape at all, it is in a direction by
no means complimentary to the persons concerned. The merchants are set down as
adventurers, with whom smuggling is a habit,
men of few scruples, violent, and ever ready
to plunge the mother-country into war to

serve their personal ends. Missionaries are characterized as indiscreet, officious, over-zealous, and peculiarly partial to appeals to the persuasive powers of the "inevitable gunboat;" whilst consuls and naval commanders are regarded as much too apt to abet both classes of residents, instead of restraining them within legitimate limits. It is nevertheless imagined that notwithstanding these adverse circumstances, contact with foreigners is on the whole humanizing and improving the Chinese, and that an appreciation of the benefits of Western civilization and progress has taken fast hold of their minds, and must in due time bear useful fruit.

It will be seen from the following pages that, although some of these notions may have had their basis in fact, yet others of them are entirely unfounded, whilst none can be accepted without qualification. Foreign residents in China will be shown to represent their native countries somewhat more worthily than they have had credit for. Several of the customs of the Chinese which come more immediately under the observation of their foreign visitors will be described, and an attempt made to prove that, with a few drawbacks of character, they exhibit many interesting and even commendable traits ; and a few remarks will then be ventured upon in conclusion as to the results of the intercommunication between the two races thus far, and as to the hopes which may be entertained in respect to the future.

CHAPTER II.

POSITION OF FOREIGNERS IN CHINA.

TRADITION and reading together have doubtless familiarized the minds of most Englishmen with the general outline of the history of our past intercourse with China, and rendered it needless to do more here than pass briefly in review the more prominent features which have marked its course down to the present date. How that centuries ago adventurous travellers visited the country at rare intervals, and brought away those tales of its fabulous wealth, the barbaric magnificence of its court, the high, but quaint civilization of its people, and the excellence as well as oddity of its wares, which have formed the framework of our notions about China ever since. How that after awhile, Spanish, Portuguese, and other navigators carried their clumsy but wonderful craft into Chinese ports, and laid the foundation of a commercial intercourse, whilst by their acts they sowed those first

seeds of ill-will and distrust, the lamentable
fruit of which we are reaping in these days.
How that later on the British East India
Company extended its agencies to Canton,
and founded a trade which for success and
mutual confidence has scarcely been surpassed.
How that with this trade opium crept in to
be a valuable commodity of traffic, becoming
in after years, incidentally with other causes,
the bone of contention that plunged China
into her first war with a European power.
How that the struggle which ensued resulted
in the freedom of British subjects from native
jurisdiction, and the establishment of five
centres of trade in the place of one, Canton,
as had been the case up to that time. And
how that sundry disputes and hostilities super-
vened from time to time, which eventually
culminated in a second and third war, that
secured for us not only an extension of trading
privileges, but the right of ministerial representation at the Chinese metropolis, Peking,
as at this moment enjoyed.

And here it may be remarked parentheti-
cally that the succession of collisions with
Western powers, which has marked the history

of China during the past thirty years, has done her grievous harm. They have gradually but effectually undermined the prestige of the ruling powers, and so have led directly to the series of devastating rebellions which have ravaged the country of late years, sapped its resources, and brought the government to the helpless condition in which it now practically lies. It may be argued that the responsibility of this result lies not so much with foreign powers as with the Chinese, whose extravagant assumptions, obstructive efforts, and want of good faith, in every instance induced the collisions which followed. To a certain extent this may be true. But it must be maintained that we—I say we, for after all England has been the chief actor on the scene—have been to blame, in that, when collision was inevitable, the operations were not so carried through as that the lesson taught should be effectual, leaving little or no likelihood of a repetition on the part of the assailed of their previous misapprehension or misconduct. It has been our misfortune, in every desultory act of hostility against local Chinese officials, as well as in every more serious process of war with the nation itself, always to stop contented with a momentary success, leave, as it were, the coping-stone of the fabric unlaid, and then to withdraw the pressure just when it was beginning to tell, credulously taking it for granted in either instance that the pledges extorted by a temporary violence would be faithfully kept.

An example or two in which this unhappy fatality betrayed itself will suffice by way of illustration. When Captain Elliot attacked the city of Canton in 1840–41, after the repudiation by the Emperor of the truce which his minister (Keshen) had agreed to in the Pei Ho River, on the condition that the British squadron should forthwith return to the South, he easily succeeded, through the valour of our sailors and soldiers, in driving the enemy from every stronghold round the city in a few hours' time, and this notwithstanding the choicest of the Tartar and Chinese troops of that day had been congregated from all parts of the country for the express purpose of defying our pretensions, and " sweeping " us from the soil of China. And how did our representative use this happy success? By entering

the city of Canton, so long proclaimed as being
too sacred for the foot of the foul foreigner,
and occupying it until the arrogant assumption had been withdrawn and redress obtained ?
By no means. He accepted overtures of peace
outside the walls, whilst actually contemplating
them as limits of a forbidden precinct, and
withdrew his forces for a handsome pecuniary
indemnity, leaving the Chinese to crow over
their success, and the identical work to be
done all over again many years after, at the
expense of a vast amount of blood and treasure. The mistake was repeated under the
late Sir Henry Pottinger. He took city after
city on the coast, and routed army after army
in an incredibly short space of time, and by
appearing with a formidable squadron before
Nanking, where a foreign ship had never
before been seen, he so terrified the Chinese
that they professed themselves ready to submit
to any terms. The result was so far good, for
he exacted the famous treaty of Nanking,
which has been the basis of our extended commercial privileges since ; but Sir H. Pottinger,
too, withdrew his forces at the moment of
triumph, and was deluded by his wily anta-

gonists into shifting the scene of detailed
negotiations back, as of old, to Canton, instead
of onwards to Peking, thereby sacrificing all
the practical benefits which had been so dearly
purchased on both sides. In the wars of 1858
and 1860, which followed as an only natural
consequence, our diplomacy was attended with
similarly untoward results. The ready acceptance by the late Lord Elgin in the first
instance of overtures of peace whilst yet short
of Peking, ended, as is well known, in the
fearful catastrophe of Taku, which convinced
Lord Elgin that the blow, to be effectual, must
be struck at the capital. The accustomed
courage and strategy of our forces brought
him there without difficulty; but he contented
himself with occupying only one gate of the
beleaguered metropolis as a temporary measure,
and, like his predecessors, he, too, hurried
away to claim the merit of his success, leaving
undetermined the crucial question of access to
the Emperor, which in the eyes of the Chinese
is the one all-important turning point of their
dispute with foreigners as to international relations; and the solution of which may yet
have to be arrived at through the expenditure

of still more blood and treasure. It were
needless here to discuss the arguments which
have been adduced in support of the necessity
of that precipitate withdrawal of our forces
from Peking, and the expediency of leaving
the audience question unsolved. I simply
state the fact, and deprecate the too probable
consequences.

Far better would it have been, both in the
interest of China and in ours, had the earliest
blow been struck home whilst she was yet
comparatively strong, and had her rulers and
people been taught in those days, whilst the
court had not yet succumbed to the influences
of luxury and vice, and corruption had not yet
wholly demoralized the administrative departments, that intercourse with the foreigner, if
accepted at all, must be accepted on conditions
of entire equality and universality. China
possessed then many master minds, who had
not yet lost the traditions of the vigorous and
patriotic rule which had marked the reigns of
the earlier Emperors of this dynasty, and the
more complete contact with foreign progress
and civilization, which would undoubtedly
have ensued upon more efficiently conducted

operations, would, I am convinced, have had
better appreciation and utilization at the
hands of the statesmen of that day than it is
unfortunately receiving now.

To return to the position in which foreigners
find themselves in China at this moment. It
has been mentioned how that residence for
the purposes of commercial intercourse at
certain ports or depôts was the result of the
last two treaties. There are fourteen in all,
eleven situated at intervals along a coast
line of 1800 miles, and three on the river
Yangtsze. In this category I do not include
Hong Kong, which is a British colony, and
consequently on an entirely different footing.
At some of these ports settlers have acquired
land for building purposes as opportunity
may have offered, and the result is that their
dwellings lie isolated and scattered about here
and there. At others a particular site has
been set apart within which the foreign
merchants are permitted to acquire property
and build, subject to an insignificant rental to
the Emperor as lord of the soil. At others
again, the later acquired ports more especially,
a concession has been made to the British

crown of a special tract subject to a trifling rental to the Chinese Government, and this has been divided into convenient lots to suit purchasers, subject to a lien on the land and all property standing thereon for a crown rental and any taxes which the majority of the settlers may agree to levy for municipal purposes. In the last two cases of course facilities have been enjoyed and largely taken advantage of for laying out the sites upon attractive and commodious plans, and considerable success has been attained in some instances in erecting settlements which combine architectural beauty with commercial convenience, and even with appliances for health and recreation. Not very many cities can vie with Shanghae, for instance, in the attractiveness and extent of the front view from the approach to it up the river, and in its streets may be seen public and private buildings equal in style and importance to those that grace European towns. Gas has been laid down for some time past, and the inhabitants have now under consideration the introduction of a system of drainage and water supply upon an extensive scale and scientific principles, which, when complete, will go far towards rendering Shanghae the healthiest and most agreeable residence in the East.   All this has been due not to Governmental aid from home, or to the action of the Chinese authorities upon the spot, but to the perseverance and enterprise, individual and general, of the foreign settlers themselves. Municipal affairs are conducted by a council elected yearly from amongst the residents, and the importance of the trust committed to their charge may be appreciated by the fact that the budget presented for acceptance at the last annual meeting exhibited a total estimated receipt for taxes, dues, licences, post office, &c., of over 60,000*l.*   This is in Shanghae alone; other ports do not of course boast a similar importance and wealth.   But at each much has been done to secure conveniences and advantages commensurate with the wants and capabilities of the place.

In the matter of amusement and recreation there is no lack, even at the smaller ports. Wherever Europeans and Americans congregate together at a distance from home, be the locality ever so remote and inhospitable, they

are certain to hit upon some method of finding
an outlet for their exuberant spirits. Shanghae
is abundantly provided in this particular.
There is a capital Club House, which from the
habit everyone indulges in of visiting it at
dusk, after a drive, ride, or walk, has also
come to be the Exchange of the place, where
business is discussed over a friendly glass of
sherry. There is a splendid Masonic Hall,
which although not exactly erected for purposes of recreation, possesses amongst its extensive suite of rooms a lofty and capacious public
hall, which is frequently appropriated to balls
and concerts. There is a Philharmonic Society,
the performers in which, albeit mere amateurs,
treat the public to concerts and promenade
music that would gratify the most accomplished taste. There is a racecourse, one of
the largest and most perfect in the East.
There are newspapers, theatres, libraries, reading and lecture associations, fives and racket
clubs, billiard-rooms, bowling-alleys, gymna-
siums, and indeed most, if not all, other of the
sources of amusement which usually distinguish the thriving well-to-do town at home.

The police arrangements, which, were

treaty principles carried out in their integrity, would properly fall to the share of the Chinese authorities, have been entirely taken in hand by the settlers themselves, and they boast a highly-paid and efficient body of men selected from amongst our London constabulary, who, although numbering but seventy in all, are wonderfully successful in maintaining order amongst the 70,000 Chinese who live within the foreign precincts. The roads are macadamized upon the principle so long adopted in England, and the traffic of carriages, breaks, and vehicles of all kinds, is quite sufficient, especially of an evening, to keep foot-passengers on the *qui vive*.

As regards religious privileges, the resident of Shanghae has nothing to complain of. The church was projected in days when money circulated far more freely than it does now, and it is therefore in size and style everything that a large and wealthy congregation could desire; but the community of the present day are paying the penalty of their predecessors' extravagant ideas, in having to forego the luxury of a steeple, until time and circumstance shall mayhap pave the way towards the possibility of a further outlay. There are two other churches, one especially devoted to seamen, and a congregational chapel, all likewise constructed and supported, with their respective ministers, by the liberality of the foreign residents. These remarks apply, as before, only to Shanghae; but other parts have their share of similar appliances for the public benefit in a social point of view.

CHAPTER III.

CHARACTER AND HABITS OF FOREIGN RESIDENTS IN CHINA.

MUCH misconception appears to prevail as to the character of foreign residents in China, a misconception which has unfortunately been intensified of late by the condemnatory tone which the home press has taken up in respect to our relations with the Chinese during the past four years. Communities in China may be roughly divided into two main sections or classes, merchants and missionaries, and to these may be added as necessary concomitants the consular and customs authorities and unemployed persons or vagrants.

The term "merchant," as applied to our countrymen in China, has been so long and so constantly associated with traffic in opium, and the alleged obtrusion of it upon the Chinese by force, that it has become in England almost a synonym for "adventurer," and even "smuggler," and the press has at times likewise distinguished it by such epithets as " rapacious," "aggressive," &c. It is unnecessary to enter here into the question of the morality or otherwise of the opium traffic ; suffice it to say that no man who has the slightest spark of philanthropy in his heart but must deprecate the existence of the trade, and regret that the production of the drug in British territory is for the time being a political necessity, or that civilized and Christian traders must needs be the means of introducing it amongst a heathen people. But it is essential that the reader should dismiss from his mind the impression that opium is smuggled into, or forced upon, the country, or that any moral turpitude of necessity attaches to the man who deals in the drug. Even in the days of its strict prohibition by the Chinese Government there were certain inlets for its introduction at various points on the coast, which were recognized for a consideration by the local authorities, and known to exist by the higher officials, who simply satisfied their sense of duty by periodical memorials to the throne and fulminations against the trade. True, one of these latter, the famous Commissioner Lin, carried his indignation and

patriotism to such a pitch as to impound the
entire stock of opium then in the Chinese
waters, and hence arose the assumption, which
has since taken so strong a hold on the public
mind, that the war which shortly after ensued
was waged with the unrighteous object of
forcing opium upon the Chinese; whereas the
claim for the property arbitrarily seized was
but one out of several grounds of complaint
which then called for redress.

The importation has of late years been legalized by treaty, and the drug is now being so
extensively produced by the Chinese upon
their own soil as sensibly to affect the demand
for the Indian-grown commodity. It is a
mistake to suppose, as many do, or to maintain,
as the American press is apt to do, that the
importation is confined to British firms alone.
They have the larger share of the trade in
their hands, as they have of every other
branch of commerce in the country; but
there are few, if any, members of other nationalities who can afford to throw a stone at
" John Bull " in the matter.   But be they
who they may on whom the responsibility
rests, it cannot be asserted that the association

involves any more demoralization of character to the individual than a connection with the beer, wine, or liquor trade is found to do in this country. On the contrary, anyone who knows anything of the leading merchants in China must have discovered from experience that in intelligence, integrity, worth, and liberality, they come behind none of the so-called merchant princes of Great Britain.

As regards the mercantile residents in China generally, it is almost an impertinence to advocate their innocence of some of the characteristics which have been ascribed to them. Commercial integrity is perhaps as much the rule with them as with communities of the same class and like importance in this country. As for any tendency to be aggressive against the Chinese, it does not need much consideration to be convinced of the fact that a state of war cannot possibly promote the pecuniary interests of any honest well-established commercial firm, whilst there is little opportunity for the development of individual aggressiveness, inasmuch as a British supreme court has been established at Shanghae, with branch provincial courts at the ports, and the Chinese are only too ready to use all the niceties of English law in the defence of their rights. Other treaty powers are more or less similarly represented, so that a Chinese need rarely, if ever, lack redress from wrong done to him by a foreigner. Unfortunately as much cannot be said, were the case transposed. The native system of procedure is at once so clumsy and faulty, and corruption is so rife in every court, high and low, whilst official antipathy against the foreigner exerts so strong an influence, that redress against a Chinese, be the case civil or criminal, is only to be obtained after persistent pressure, and frequently cannot be secured at all.

So much for the character of the foreign merchant in China.

His habits are very much what they are at home. He builds himself a mansion in the handsomest style that his firm or himself can afford, and he furnishes it as a rule with home-made furniture, plate, glass, &c., all of the best quality. For his business requirements through the day the Shanghae resident generally keeps a Norwich car, brougham, or some other convenient kind of vehicle, in which to traverse the settlement in all its parts. For evening exercise, if a subordinate, he goes to cricket or rackets, or bowls, or takes a gallop on a pet pony, or trots out his dog-cart or phaeton. If a head of house or a married man, he drives out some more pretentious vehicle with a pair of Cape, Australian, or Californian horses; nearly everybody drives or rides, and he must be a struggling creature who cannot muster an animal or vehicle of some kind. After the evening airing comes dinner, and it is at this meal that the foreign resident in China concentrates his efforts to forget that he is an exile from home. The native markets abound with fish, meat, poultry, and vegetables, and the foreigner's own carefully-kept poultry-yard, pigsty, dairy, and kitchen garden assist materially in supplying him with luxuries not procurable of the same quality amongst the Chinese. Of stores, such as those known at home as oilman's stores, he has no lack, for he imports all these from England, and there are foreign shops on the spot which abound in delicacies of all kinds, supplied to them wholesale by Fortnum and Mason, Crosse

and Blackwell, and other large grocery establishments in this country. Wines of superior
quality are as a rule placed on the table, all
of course imported from England; and malt
liquors abound in every variety. Shanghae
can even boast its own brewery, in which
an old enterprising resident, Mr. Evans,
has succeeded, after years of effort, in producing ale and porter not to be surpassed
in quality and flavour by the famous home
brews. It may be imagined therefore that, as
far as the material is concerned, the table of
the foreign merchant need not suffer much in
comparison with the board of any well-to-do
gentleman at home.

Hospitality is generally and liberally practised, especially towards casual visitors from
other parts of the world; and it is a rare
table which is not often surrounded by a
genial chatty circle of friends.

Society has, however, always suffered a
great drawback in the paucity of ladies; but
this want is being rapidly repaired, for a
marrying mania has taken possession of our
so-called Chinese bachelors of late, so that
there are few who visit England but return

Benedicts. It is a fortunate circumstance that it is so, for although our countrymen in China are, as has been described, good men enough in themselves, still they are not such commendable characters but that they need the presence of woman to humanize them, and to counteract the demoralizing influences which are inseparable from association with inferior races, and absence from home ties and checks. Any fair ladies who may contemplate going out to China, may safely assure themselves that their lot need not be at all a subject of commiseration with their friends. Ladies in China, from their very paucity, are made so much of, that it needs all the discretion of which they are capable to sustain the ordeal altogether unharmed, and the style of life is such that, as has been explained, but for the immediate surroundings of people, scenery, and so on, they need never be oppressed by the thought that they are residents in a comparatively barbarous country.

The domestic servants are wonderfully good and clever in adapting themselves to foreign notions. They are of course Chinese, and men are employed, not women, unless it be

for ladies'-maids and nurses. They are always
called "Boys." There is generally a head,
or house-boy, who corresponds to our butler
at home, and performs very much the same
duties; under him come from two to three
younger men, called "No. 2 Boys," who look
after one's wardrobe, attend at table, answer
the bell, and so on. In larger establishments,
the "head boy" is allowed to bring in one
or two of his younger relatives, or friends,
who are called "learn-pidgeon," *i.e.* apprentices, and who make themselves useful as
pages, whilst they learn their trade. For
housemaids men are employed, called "coolies,"
a lower class of servant, but none the less
intelligent and useful. The kitchen is also
presided over by a man, who has from two to
four mates under him, the real artists in most
cases. One may live in China for years, and
be perfectly satisfied all the while with the
style and skill with which his viands are
served up, without ever making the acquaintance of his *chef de cuisine*. The fact is that a
good cook will often serve half-a-dozen establishments, receiving wages from each, and
each employer congratulating himself upon

the possession of an admirable artist, whilst all the while the man is simply educating a number of mates and apprentices, who in the course of time become *chefs* in their turn. They cook, of course, in the best English and French styles. I have seen dinners and banquets laid out in China that would do credit to home tables. If there be anything that a Chinese has a special gift for, it is cooking.

They are, moreover, the handiest servants in the world in case of pressure or emergency. A master of a house has often occasion to send for his butler late in the afternoon, and tell him that a number of guests will be in at dinner that evening. The simple answer is " Very well, sir ; " and when the hour arrives, there is the dinner, which, as far as abundance or cookery goes, might very well have been ordered some days beforehand. It is also very much the habit, in the winter months, for gentlemen to go in parties up country shooting, and first-rate sport they have, with pheasants, partridges, deer, pig, wild-fowl, &c., free from the trammels of preserves, licences, or game-laws. They go in cosily-furnished house-boats, in which they

spend a week or a fortnight at a time. On
these occasions the Chinese servant is invaluable. The cook, "boy," and "coolie," generally accompany the party, and, although the
space is somewhat cramped, still they succeed
in providing their masters with meals and
comforts precisely as if they were at home on
shore, and this without a word of grumbling
or discontent. In short, when well selected
and managed, and when kindly treated, the
Chinese "boy" will perhaps match any
servant in the world for activity, docility,
honesty, and general usefulness. The women
servants are equally good in their way.
Ladies find them invaluable, and for the care
of children they are particularly well suited,
being mild, patient, gentle, and kindly to a
fault.

I have dwelt thus much upon the characteristics of the servants employed by foreigners,
not only to show how they fare in this
particular, but because these servants are the
only natives with whom the foreign merchant
comes more immediately into contact. The
opinion prevalent at home that foreigners
mingle in Chinese society generally is alto-

gether a mistaken one. The conventional rules of the Chinese are so constituted, and their habits of thought and customs so peculiar, that there is little or no encouragement to court acquaintance on either part, even were the entire ignorance of each other's language not to present a serious bar in the way of an interchange of ideas. There is a class of Chinese brokers and middle-men who haunt the offices of the merchants, but they are mostly shrewd clever upstarts, whom the difficulties of interlingual communication have introduced into the trade, and, with rare exceptions, they lay no claim to respectability, even with the Chinese themselves. The language employed between these brokers and the merchants is a jargon made up of English, Portuguese, Chinese, and Malay words, tortured into unrecognizable shapes and constructions, and it is little fitted to sustain any conversation beyond what appertains to the mere technicalities of trade. I have frequently expressed to our merchants the opinion that it is a pity they do not take the trouble to learn the Chinese language. Its acquirement in the spoken form to an extent sufficient for

all practical purposes offers no difficulties that
an average intellect and a moderate share of
determination cannot surmount, and familiarity with it would have the effect of freeing
the foreigner from the domination of roguish
brokers and compradores, at whose mercy he
now lies, whilst it would open the way to a
more extended acquaintance and friendly
intercourse to the mutual advantage of both
parties.   There is perhaps no country in the
world, frequented by the English-speaking
race, in which merchants are so lamentably
ignorant of the customs and resources of the
locality in which they live as they are at this
moment in China, and this is entirely to be
attributed to a want of familiarity with the
language.

CHAPTER IV.

MISSIONARIES IN CHINA.

AFTER the merchants of China, the missionaries next claim attention as an important element of foreign society. In approaching this part of my subject, I wish to premise that I have no sympathy with those who, for want of consideration or from mere prejudice, think lightly of the work and character of the missionary. The man who honestly devotes his life and energies to the instruction of the poor and ignorant at home, or to the conversion of benighted heathen abroad, must always merit the profound respect of every right-minded individual. It does not need my feeble testimony to sustain the assertion that there have been and now are many such devoted men of all denominations of the Christian Church labouring in China, and if I venture in any way to criticise the body, it is not from any lack of appreciation of its high and sacred objects, but simply because missionaries are human, and there cannot but be many things in which those who look at their proceedings from another standpoint than their own, must find occasion for dissent or remark.

Missionaries in China, like their co-religionists in the West, are divided into two principal sections, Romanist and Protestant; and the latter are again subdivided, unhappily, into denominations numerous enough to puzzle their fellow-Christians, let alone the heathen to whom they are accredited. It is very much the fashion with persons who are only too glad to find occasion for complaint against Protestant missionaries to subject them to an unreasoning comparison with their Romanist brethren, much to the discredit of the former. This is, to say the least, unfair. The two classes of labourers go out under such diametrically opposite systems of church organization and discipline, and they pursue their objects in such entirely different methods, that no comparison, except as regards the several results of their labours, can be either just or accurate, and this it is next to impossible to institute to any satisfactory degree. Even

to attempt it would be to launch upon a sea
of controversy as to what constitutes a convert, and which is nearer the right, Romanist
or Protestant. I shall make it my endeavour
to avoid such invidious comparisons as much
as possible, preferring to treat of both parties
in their several relations to the people amongst
whom they labour.

The Romanist missionaries one sees but
little of, although, as compared to the Protes-
tants, their name is legion. Their system is
to penetrate deeply into the interior the
moment they arrive, to disassociate themselves
entirely from the mercantile classes of foreigners, and to work disguised as natives, unob-
trusively and unremittingly, at the various
stations which have been occupied by them
for years; in some cases, for centuries. Their
devotion is as remarkable as their success has
been astonishing, and I am one of those who
believe that they have been the means of
accomplishing and still do accomplish a vast
amount of good. They rely mainly upon
educational means for securing adherents, and
although the process must necessarily be a
slow one, yet the results, when these come

D

to exhibit themselves, are certainly more satisfactory as regards the number and permanency
of the conversions.   Wherever a Romanist
missionary station is found in a town or village,
it is sure to be a nucleus of a more or less
extended circle of Christian families, in many
of which the faith has been handed down
from generation to generation, and I have
been often struck by the quiet and respectability which prevails amongst such communities
as compared to the heathen around them, as
also by the respect and attachment shown
by them towards their "spiritual fathers," as
the priests are usually termed.

   It was, I think, an unfortunate incident
in the history of Roman Catholic missions,
and, by association, in that of Christian missions in China generally, when the French
Government initiated the measure of exacting
toleration of Christianity from the Chinese as
a treaty right.   It has had the effect of with-
drawing the Romanist labourers from the
seclusion which until then had been a necessity, of emboldening them to claim the resti-
tution of properties and privileges which had
long ago been forfeited on political grounds,

and of encouraging them latterly even to go the length of asserting judicial rights over the native members of their churches, and seeking to release them from their fealty to their proper sovereign. As a natural consequence of such high-handed proceedings, the jealousy of the Chinese Government has been roused against foreign propagandism in general, a sympathetic enmity has taken hold of the minds of the influential classes and literati, and both have not been slow to profit by the occasion to incite the entire population against foreigners and their faith. Hence the agitations, persecutions, and massacres, which have left their bloody mark upon the relations of the past few years, and which are but a foretaste, it is to be feared, of what we may yet have to mourn in the future.

Protestant missionaries pursue their object, as has been remarked, upon a wholly different principle. They go out as a rule married, and the majority settle at the open ports, where they build themselves foreign houses, for the most part, in or near the concessions common to all foreign residents, and mix more or less in the foreign society of each place.

They are careful to disclaim the possession of
a common object or interest with the merchants amongst whom they live; nevertheless
it cannot but be that the natives fail to give
them credit for the self-sacrificing character of
their mission, and that as a consequence they
lose a certain amount of influence and respect.
As regards their married condition, I am not
by any means prepared to condemn it, or to
advocate celibacy as a rule, for I know of
many devoted couples, whose united and
energetic efforts have been productive of great
good.   At the same time I venture to think
that a man or woman labouring single-handed
must of necessity prove a more effective missionary as far as China is concerned, for not
only is increased leisure afforded for undivided
attention to the work, but more opportunity
and freedom are given for complete disassocia-
tion from foreign surroundings, and a thorough
seclusion amongst the natives; and there is a
greater likelihood moreover of earning the
good-will and respect of the Chinese, in whose
eyes celibacy constitutes an important element
of self-sacrifice.

The Protestant missionaries, save in the case

of one particular denomination, retain their dress and national habits, and they are right. Disguise, although so universally and successfully employed by the Romanists, must be regarded as objectionable. It is calculated to lower the individual in the opinion of the natives, and where it is employed, as in the exceptional case alluded to, by the female members of the mission likewise, the effect is even more mischievous.

The Protestant missionaries, again, have shown no inclination to indulge the extravagant pretensions which have been ascribed to their Romanist co-labourers in regard to the withdrawal of converts from native jurisdiction. I have found, it is true, in my consular relations with them, a tendency to believe their converts always to be in the right, whenever a dispute has occurred with the heathen or the mandarins : but this is a pardonable weakness, which is easily accounted for under the circumstances, and any evil results likely to arise out of it can always be checked by the disinterested view which the Consul should take of the matter when brought to his cognizance. Our missionaries have also

been charged with habitual indiscretion in the
conduct of their proceedings, and a too ready
leaning towards advocacy of coercive measures
whenever thwarted. That some of them are
at times indiscreet, may be granted; for, as a
rule, they are not men of the world, and their
minds are apt to be warped by the engrossing
character of their pursuits. But it must be
denied that they exhibit any settled partiality
for recourse to force. They are by treaty
entitled to full protection in the pursuit of
their avocations, to say nothing of special
stipulations which make propagandism lawful,
and where they find reason to imagine that
these rights are being interfered with, what
more natural than that they should appeal to
the Consul for assistance in the maintenance
of such rights? It is for him to consider how
far remonstrance on his part is called for, and
it will be found in every instance of what are
called missionary troubles, that this process has
been carefully followed out.

I am not in a position to state definitively
what are the results of Protestant missionary
labour amongst the Chinese so far. Their
practice of only reckoning as converts those

adults whom they conscientiously believe to have been brought to a saving knowledge of the truth, reduces their statistics of proselytism to a very material extent; but even with this check, and taking into consideration, on the one hand, the limited number of labourers, and, on the other, the difficulty of bringing the Chinese mind to appreciate abstract religious truths independently of sensational influences, I think I am only doing the Protestant missionaries simple justice when I state that their efforts have been attended with exceptional success, and this although it is but a short while ago since they ceased to count their converts by mere hundreds.

Their progress might have been yet more marked, in my opinion, could they have been content to leave denominational differences at home, and could they have avoided the unhappy controversies in respect to the best rendering of the term for GOD, which have not only occasioned disunion amongst themselves, but have tended to confuse the minds of the natives as to the character and attributes of the Deity.

They have erred likewise in other points

which it is necessary to call attention to as
bearing upon their influence with the natives.
One is a propensity to erect pretentious
churches after the foreign style of architecture,
with tall steeples or towers that show out
obtrusively over the uniformly low roofs of a
Chinese city. These towers are apt to create
ill-will in an entire population, the Chinese idea
being that any erection pointing upwards,
unless it be one of their own propitiatory
pagodas, is calculated to bring down evil influences productive of ill fortune, disease, and
death, upon the entire neighbourhood. A
Chinaman is, moreover, a timid creature, and it
is my belief that for one stranger who would
hesitate to enter a common-place native building supposed to be tenanted or used by a
foreigner, three would shrink from being seen
to approach a construction the very architecture of which would indicate its strange and
obnoxious purpose. Not that the Protestant
missionaries are alone open to criticism in this
particular. Since the governmental toleration
of Christianity, secured by the Romanists under
the French treaty, they have been much too
forward in marking concessions made to them

of plots formerly theirs by erecting thereon cathedrals of obtrusive size and style of architecture, offending thereby not only the superstitions, but the religious prejudices of the natives, who naturally object to see Christian places of worship raised upon sites for generations sacred to their own heathen shrines.

Another mistake which the Protestant missionaries have made is in confining their efforts too exclusively to the acquirement of local *patois* of the language, and to the production therein of tracts and translations of the Scriptures; the result, as regards the natives, being very much what might be imagined in England were foreign propagandists to attempt to preach and distribute books in a Somersetshire, Yorkshire, cockney, or any other dialect. Some missionaries, in their over-estimate of the difficulty of acquiring the written Chinese language for themselves, or of getting illiterate Chinese to master it with sufficient facility to become readers of their books within a reasonable space of time, have even hit upon the novel expedient of inventing a new written medium, by " Romanizing," as they call it, the Chinese language, that is, expressing it phonetically by means of our alphabetical system, and schools are now taught and books published in this hybrid character. It is argued that, owing to the comparative ease with which this mode of writing Chinese is acquired, it becomes the means of enabling the simplest child or oldest crone to read the Bible in the native tongue after a few lessons, a feat neither could otherwise accomplish. And to a certain extent this is true. But it stands to reason that for every child or old woman who may thus be won over, there must be hundreds of thousands left totally unreached, and the system must therefore fail of general or practical utility. As regards preaching or teaching in a local *patois*, it may secure attention and apprehension amongst the lower classes in a particular neighbourhood, but the speaker, unless he acquire more than one *patois*—there being nearly one to every large city—must be at a manifest disadvantage elsewhere, whilst no respectable or educated person will demean himself to listen, save perhaps for curiosity's sake, to a foreigner speaking in a vulgar dialect.

The same argument applies with even more force to the publication of books in the colloquial. There is perhaps no people who are more partial to reading than the Chinese, or who better appreciate beauty of composition and purity of style in their books. Until the missionaries study more than they have done to gratify this taste, their publications must fail to attract attention with the reading classes, and may even, by exciting contempt, occasion more harm than good. A Chinese statesman was not much mistaken when he observed in a late, memorial that native institutions and creeds had but little to fear from the disturbing influences of missionary publications. It is only fair I should add that there are exceptions to this rule; some few missionaries having effected real good by placing before the Chinese translations of some of our scientific works, as well as original compositions on popular subjects, all in good scholastic style, and they have been rewarded by the popularity that these works have earned in even the best circles.

In connection with the limited results of Protestant missionary teaching so far, I owe it

to the Protestant missionary body to state that
they themselves ascribe much of their want of
success to the demoralizing effects of the opium
trade, as well as to a failure on the part of
foreigners generally to support them in their
teachings by a conduct and example worthy
of the Christian profession.   It cannot be
doubted that the opium traffic has much to
answer for in the way of neutralizing missionary efforts, not only in its direct effects upon
the victims themselves, but in the hatred and
suspicion of everything foreign which it has
engendered in the minds of the natives generally.   But as regards the other counteracting
influence which the missionaries plead in bar
of success, I think they are apt to take up a
too decided opinion.   Residence in the East
and association with heathen and less civilized
races do not as a rule tend to elevate the
moral and mental standard to which the
European may have been schooled in his own
country.   But foreign residents in China are,
I think, as little affected by this demoralization,
if I may so term it, as perhaps any wanderers
into Eastern climes ; and if the Chinese take
the trouble to study them at all it is rather to

contemplate with wonder their (in the Chinese idea) *bizarre* habits and notions than to draw any deductions from their conduct in a moral point of view. Individual instances no doubt do occur in which the missionary finds himself posed by allusions to laxity of conduct in his own countrymen, but I question whether the objection seriously presents itself to the minds of the masses as an argument against Christianity.

The whole missionary question is a perplexing one. As has been already observed, the proceedings of the Romanists, although founded upon treaty rights, have tended to rouse the hitherto dormant jealousy of the Chinese Government and influential classes, and this has led to the prevalence for the moment of a state of feelings thoroughly hostile to foreigners, and which the merest accident at any point may so excite or intensify as to bring about a dangerous outbreak when least expected. It is a mistake, however, to assert, as some do, that this is but a phase of the natural antipathy with which the Chinese regard the foreigner, or to argue, as others do, that it is his faith alone which is objected to, and that all hostility would cease with the retraction of the treaty rights of toleration, and consequently of foreign intervention in support of missionaries and their adherents. To the mass of the people the position of foreigners in the country is a matter of indifference, and a foreigner may usually pass through their most crowded haunts with immunity from personal risk,* save where an impression prevails that the local authorities would wink at his being interfered with. But with the mandarins and the class to which they belong the case is different. They have never been cordial, and some of them do not care to conceal their dislike, or even hostility. This feeling, nevertheless, as far as they are concerned, has been merely personal to the foreigner and the progress he represents, and until lately has had little to do with his religion. On the contrary, it is my belief, based upon the statements of those competent to judge, that in the negotiations which immediately preceded the conclusion of the British

* An exception must be recorded against the province of Honan, the population of which has the character of being turbulent, and has generally been found inimical by foreign travellers.

treaty, the toleration clause was found to be one of those most easily pressed upon the acceptance of the Chinese Commissioners.

This comparative indifference, on the one hand, to the foreigner, and on the other to his faith, might have continued indefinitely, but for the near approach of the period when the revision of the treaties was to take place, when it was feared that innovations of all kinds would be introduced by foreigners, in the way of telegraphs, railways, and such like. The anti-foreign party felt that the very existence of their time-honoured institutions depended upon prompt action in a repellent direction. A mission was organized, on the one hand, for the express purpose of coaxing foreign powers into foregoing, for the time being, any extravagant demands, whilst on the other, the ill-advised pretensions of the Romanists, and their practice of collecting infants for their orphanages, were each in its way made a pretext for disseminating all kinds of evil stories against foreigners generally. The result has shown with how much of success this has been effected, more perhaps than the projectors at all anticipated. The

Government has since professed its inability
to stem the torrent, the floodgates of which,
by means of a temporizing and feeble policy,
it had been indirectly instrumental in opening ; whilst it has proposed, by way of solution
of the difficulty, that propagandism by foreigners should be placed on a different footing for
the future.   The Chinese officials are rather
prone thus to allow a desired public opinion
to grow into shape, and even to venture to
encourage its formation by the employment
of governmental appliances, and then to affect
an inability to pursue any corrective policy
that may be suggested, on the plea that the
very opinion which they have been to a certain extent the means of creating is too deeply
rooted to be lightly overruled.

It would be out of place for me to suggest
the best means of meeting the emergency.
I will only venture to deprecate sincerely the
retraction of any existing treaty stipulations.
It would simply be to play directly into the
hands of those of the Chinese whose cherished
object is not so much to crush the missionary,
as to expel, or at any rate, to restrict the
foreigner ; to endanger the whole fabric of

treaty relations, which has been erected at
the cost of so much blood and treasure; and
to plunge us possibly into yet deeper com-
plications. The treaty I believe to be entirely equal to the satisfactory solution of
any difficulties which a missionary might
perchance occasion by his excess of zeal or
indiscretion.

CHAPTER V.

CONSULS AND CUSTOMS AUTHORITIES, ETC.

HAVING thus discussed the Mercantile and Missionary sections of the foreign communities in China, it only remains to say a word or two respecting the other classes of foreign residents alluded to, namely, the vagrants and the Consular and Custom House authorities.

The vagrant or destitute foreigners consist chiefly of deserters from ships, and mechanics who have failed in the attempt to establish themselves, or who, having established themselves in a small way, live a sort of hand-to-mouth existence upon the wants of the seafaring men resorting to the port. This class happily is not numerous, but it is worthy of notice as being a fruitful occasion of misunderstanding with the Chinese authorities, owing to their reckless and aggressive bearing towards the natives. The foreign authorities have to keep them under strict surveillance and check, and at times to proceed to the

extremity of deporting them from the country,
for which purpose, in the case of the British,
special powers are given by local ordinances.
At Shanghae a refuge has been instituted
by voluntary contribution and with Consular
co-operation, and it is calculated to do much
good in ridding society of this dangerous
class.

Of Consular officials it does not befit me to
say much, being myself a member of that
body. I owe it, however, to my fellow-officials
to state, that they are zealous and hard-work-
ing servants of the Crown (I am now speaking
of my own countrymen), and that they merit
all the confidence that the Government and
the public can give them. Unlike our Consular agents in European and other countries,
they are charged with important judicial
functions under the Supreme Court at Shanghae, and, although in all international matters
they are entirely accountable to H.M.'s Minister at Peking, they nevertheless are regarded
by the Chinese to some extent as representative
functionaries, and practically they exercise
considerable diplomatic influence in the several
districts to which they are accredited. From

the distance at which they are removed from
their immediate superiors, and the urgency
of the demand made upon their action when
needed, they are constantly placed in circumstances which call for the exercise of all their
faculties in the loyal and discreet solution of
difficulties, and I think the instances are rare
in which they have shown themselves unequal
to an emergency. There has been a tendency
of late with the press to characterize our Consuls
as officious, as aggressive, as fond of indulging
a little brief authority, and as being too ready
to claim naval assistance in the adjustment of
questions. But these are the random verdicts
of individuals who do not know our Consuls,
and are simply ignorant of the difficulties by
which they are beset. These latter cannot be
fully entered into here, but something of their
nature may be imagined from the fact that
British Consuls have on the one hand to satisfy
the clamourings of their countrymen for the
full enjoyment of privileges under a treaty,
the penal stipulations of which Consular authority is so fully empowered, as well as
stringently compelled, to enforce, whilst on the
other hand they find themselves met by the

Chinese authorities in a spirit which goes far towards neutralizing their efforts to carry out that treaty on principles of justice to both parties. The above remarks entirely apply to the Consuls-General and Consuls of other Treaty Powers besides Great Britain, save in the matter of accountability to the British Minister and Supreme Court.

The Customs officials are foreign employés under the Chinese Government. The system was introduced years ago by Consul (now Sir Rutherford) Alcock, at Shanghae. He found his efforts to enforce strict adherence to the tariff on the part of British merchants so entirely frustrated by the collusion of the native Customs officials with a few of the less scrupulous amongst the community, that he suggested to the Chinese the introduction of a foreign element into their Customs staff, and they fell in with the proposition forthwith. The experiment, commenced in the first instance at Shanghae, was found to be attended with such success in protecting the revenue from fraud, that the Chinese were glad to extend it to all the open ports, and a regular service has thus grown into being, which is superintended by a British Inspector-General at Peking, and officered, even down to tide-waiters, by foreigners of all nations; a thoroughly able and well-educated body of men. Their perfect acquaintance with the language, the acquirement of which is made a condition of advancement, the intimate relations in which they stand by virtue of their functions towards the Chinese Government and authorities, and the confidence with which these officers have been treated by the Governments to which they severally belong, as well as by their own countrymen, have all combined to place the foreign Customs staff, and more especially its leaders, on a splendid vantage ground for convincing the Chinese that their true interest lies in extending and consolidating their intercourse with foreign nations, and in encouraging the admission into the country of a more lively progress, and more advanced civilization than their own. For all that I can assert to the contrary, efforts may not have been wanting on their part to promote these desirable objects, and something has been done towards meeting the requirements of the trade by the construction of a few lighthouses, beacons, &c., on the coast; but the general results so far certainly warrant me in stating that the magnificent opportunities thus enjoyed have not by any means been improved as they might have been. A late issue of 'The Times' newspaper has given publicity to the translation of a memorial which the Inspector-General, Mr. Hart, has addressed to the Chinese throne, calling attention to errors in the domestic and foreign policies of the nation, and suggesting a more enlightened course of action in the interest equally of China as of Foreign Powers. I hail this representation as a step in the right direction; but I none the less regret that efforts of the kind were not commenced at an earlier period, and not more persistently carried out since.

CHAPTER VI.

CUSTOMS OF THE CHINESE.—SHOP SIGNS.

THE first thing that must attract the eye of an observant stranger, upon finding himself in a Chinese town, presuming him to have recovered from the effects of the foul odours which always infest the crowded suburbs lining the approaches thereto, will be the picturesque vista presented by the perpetually recurring series of smart shop-signs displayed in every principal thoroughfare. The peculiar conformation of the Chinese character, and the possibility of collocating the words either in horizontal, perpendicular, or any other lines without prejudice to legibility, renders them particularly well adapted for decorative purposes; and the Chinese exhibit much taste and skill in turning this characteristic to advantage in advertising their business and wares.

The shop signs, it must be understood, are not, as with us, displayed merely upon the shop-fronts: but each establishment is furnished with projecting eaves, frequently elaborately carved and decorated, and under these at either corner next the street, is suspended or erected a perpendicular board richly varnished, and inscribed on both sides with the name of the concern and a notice of the commodities sold, so that it may be read at a distance by persons passing up or down the street: very frequently a scroll of cloth also inscribed on both sides is hung across the street for the same purpose. It is the long line of these gaudy signs, stretching overhead and on both sides, and visible at times for a full mile or more, that forms the very attractive vista above alluded to.

Shops and business houses are not known in China by the names of the proprietors or firms, as in our plain common-sense country. When Brown, Jones, and Robinson, or, to select patronymics correspondingly common in China, when King, Gold, and Stone, set up shop or commence business, they assume a style or designation, which is as a rule composed of two words, the most felicitous in their meaning that can be selected, such, for example, as "Celestial affluence," "Perpetual

success," " Overflowing abundance," &c. ; and
the concern is thenceforward known by that
title, all bills, notes, and business documents
being authenticated by its employment.

Some idea of the working of this practice
may be derived from comparing it with the
similar one common amongst the French and
other continental nations, of giving fancy
names to their establishments, such as " Au
bon diable," "Au fidèle berger," " À la corbeille
des fleurs," &c. ; the only difference being that
in the case of the Europeans the names of the
partners in the firm are employed or displayed
likewise, whereas with the Chinese they
never appear, not even in correspondence. In
many cases the same designation is proudly
retained by the family for several generations,
and not unfrequently this conceit is carried to
the length of cherishing and even exhibiting
the original old sign-board with which the
ancestors laid the foundation of the business,
religiously protected from paint or repairs.
It may seem strange that any language should
contain a sufficient number of felicitous terms
to suit the wants of the business portion of so
vast a population ; but the difficulty does not

exist in practice, and although many characters must of necessity be reiterated over, and over again in the signs of a single street, not to say town, yet so cleverly are the changes rung upon the class of characters employed, and so excellently is their distribution contrived, that it would not occur to anyone rambling through a town that any sign he observes has met his eye before.

Let me now ask the reader to accompany me in imagination on a ramble, say along the main street of Ningpo, in order to see what these signs say. Here is a remarkably handsome one, varnished jet black and inscribed with large boldly-penned characters in gold. It reads, being interpreted, "Limitless production. Feasts prepared *à la Tartare* or *à la Chinoise*," a distinction, it may be presumed, possessed of more importance to the Celestials than to their foreign visitors. "The delicacies of the season ; sea-slugs smothered in vermicelli and trimmed with finely-shred ham. Forcemeat puffs, meals of boiled rice, plain, or with cooked meats, ready at all hours." This is on one side of the shop : on the other is displayed a smaller, but not less pretentious, board, suggesting the possession of "Delicacies from beyond the seas." Peeping into the interior of the shop, may be observed another attractive but smaller sign-board, tastefully fitted in crimson and gold, which points out to the sentimental or sociable wayfarer that he may be supplied with "tête-à-tête meals to his fancy;" and on another wall is displayed the suggestive hint, also cleverly framed, that "famous wine from over the sea" is provided for thirsty customers. Each of these signs has a band of scarlet silk flaunting loosely from the handle, a token that the shop has been lately established or enlarged, or that some accession of business or capital has accrued to the firm, scarlet being the festive colour in China. Not infrequently coarse white cotton or hempcloth may be observed similarly mounted, a sign that death has invaded the establishment, white being the colour of mourning. At New Year time the sign-boards are likewise ornamented with scarlet streamers, more especially amongst the Cantonese.

Having taken a sip of their famous wine and courteously eschewed the offer of a smothered sea-slug, we will pass farther up the street.

Here are a series of showy sign-boards, backed by row upon row of heavily-tasselled glass lanterns, all prettily painted with figures of flowers and Chinese writing. It does not need any conversance with the language to discover the business done upon these premises, the odour of drugs and aromatics being sufficiently suggestive. Over the centre door are displayed two characters, meaning "Double-headed Phœnix." This, as in the case of the characters representing "Limitless production" at the eating house just alluded to, is the designation or style of the shop.

Taking its other boards in their order, the first sets forth that "Decoctions are prepared with accuracy from fragrant materials," leaving one to infer that "John Chinaman" likes his doses characteristic as well as safe. The next boasts of "Boluses, powders, ointments, and pills carefully mixed." A third announces "Drugs from every province in the empire." Then two others, by way of hint no doubt to hard bargainers, declare that "Wares will be found genuine, and prices true to value;" and that "No two prices are asked" for the same article.

The house next to the druggist's shows
sign-boards which betray the residence of a
physician, who, judging by their number and
high colouring, must be a renowned and
popular leech. We will call him Dr. Dry,
this being the British equivalent of his
Chinese surname. On the one side of his
gateway may be read " Dry *Quartus*, great
grandson of Dry *Primus*, of Ningpo, whose
spécialité is to treat fractures, contusions and
wounds, to set bones and return dislocations."
His method of performing the last-mentioned
operations is not stated, but I imagine it
would be considered somewhat unprecedented
and peculiar by our better-trained practition-
ers, judging from a reply I received from one
of these gentlemen to my inquiry as to the
mode in which he reduced a fracture : " I
simply rub the part well," he assured me,
" with a specific ointment of my own preparing, and the result is miraculous." The sign-
board upon the other side of the entrance
door repeats the practitioner's name, and
announces that he treats internal as well as
external complaints, cures affections of the
throat, administers acupuncture and the moxa,

and so on—more than it is convenient to
describe. Over the door are suspended two
complimentary slabs given to the worthy doctor, no doubt, by grateful patients. On the
one is inscribed the sentence, '" Bent arm ;
three principles," in allusion to his skill in
feeling the pulse, which in China is touched
with three fingers, the pulse in the right
wrist being regarded as intimately connected
with three of the internal organs of the human
body, and that in the left with three other
organs. Ability to feel the pulse is considered
in this country as the true criterion of medical
proficiency. The other slab has on it the
words "Excellent faculty, handed down by
family descent." Reference is here made to
the fact of the profession having been here-
ditary in the family, the practitioner's father
and grandfather having both been medical
men of renown at Ningpo. In the opinion of
the Chinese, occupation and fame derived by
inheritance afford the most reliable evidence
of professional skill where physicians are concerned.

The Chinese are a quack-ridden race, as is
evidenced by the number and size of their

druggists' shops, and the various extravagant
puffs which are exhibited upon the walls every
day. Of this, however, more anon. A pretender has only to display in front of a tented
table by the wayside " The Doctor So-and-So,
a physician and surgeon by descent for several
generations," and he will rarely lack a patient.
Prescriptions are, as with us, written and presented to the druggist for making up, and, as
used to be the case with our ancestors of old,
great faith is put in the virtues of strange
herbs, woods, and roots. The Chinese nevertheless are fully alive to the properties of many of
the most valuable drugs and medicines which
figure in our pharmacopœias. Physicians
frequently combine necromancy and fortune-
telling with the practice of medicine. I may
here mention a curious custom which prevails
everywhere in China, as regards the disposal
of the materials of which a prescription is
composed after having been made use of.
Infusions and decoctions are the favourite
remedies, and when these have been prepared
the refuse is carefully deposited in the centre
of the street or highway, a superstitious notion
being prevalent that if the mess is sniffed at

by the horse on which the spirit of the T'ien-i Star rides, the result will be certain to be favourable for the patient. The T'ien-i Star, or "Celestial cure," is supposed to have a beneficial influence upon invalids, and the spirit which inhabits it is believed to patrol the streets nightly in order to keep watch over the welfare of the inhabitants.

But to proceed with the sign-boards. There, next to the physician, is what we should call an optician, who gives out that he manufactures "crystal eye-glasses for young and old." Then comes a tobacconist, who "imports for the special use of his establishment tobacco from Fuhkien, Chefoo, and Hangchow." Conveniently posted on the opposite side of the street is a pipe-maker, who gives out that he has "pipes manufactured on purpose for his firm out of Yunnan white copper." Here again is a tallow-chandler, who "constructs dips fit for presentation as tribute to royalty." Next comes a musical instrument maker, who offers for competition organs, flutes, banjos, guitars, fiddles, and all kinds of musical instruments. Next a "Christy," who "makes caps to suit every season of the year." Then

F

a " Hoby," who " embroiders boots in the newest fashions." (The boots of a Chinese exqui-
site, it must be remembered, are made of
satin.) After him a dyer, whose " blues and
blacks rival celestial colouring." Then another
chandler, who, more pretentious than his
rival higher up the street, declares that his
wares are " double-dipped and small wick'd,"
and who even goes so far as to quote from
some poet a couplet which pictures the student
as " labouring beside the midnight lamp."
And last, for the category must be ended
somewhere, is a silk mercer, whose sign is
worth quoting in full: " We possess our own
country agencies, where selection is made for
the market of the finest sorts of silk, in the
manipulation of which neither time nor labour
is spared. We manufacture every suit of rich
and pure silk, thread and floss-silk, silk for
bow strings, tassels, and cords; we give our-
selves especially to the weaving and plaiting
of parti-coloured girdles and fittings of Court
caps in the newest Peking style. We also
make fringes for caps, handkerchiefs of all
kinds, damask or crape, head-bands and collars
of satin or gauze." Shops of this last class,

i. e. drapers, haberdashers, &c., usually have the designation printed upon the paper in which customers' purchases are wrapped, with conditions of sale attached; such as, " Customs' Barrier and transit duties payable by purchaser," " No goods exchanged or received back that have been folded, rumpled, or cut."

CHAPTER VII.

ADVERTISING IN CHINA.

THE large number of advertisements which
everywhere cover convenient walls would also
be likely to attract the eye of the foreign
visitor to a Chinese town. Advertising, although very generally had recourse to in
China, appears to be confined to particular
classes of business, such as those of druggists,
eating-houses, lodging-houses, doctors, theatrical corps, lecturers, fortune-tellers. In fact,
it is not considered quite the thing to advertise, on the principle, it is presumed, that
"good wine needs no bush." An exception
seems to be made in favour of jewellers, silk
and satin mercers, dyers, biscuit bakers,
piece-goods vendors, and one or two others,
who are permitted by the rules of conven-
tionality to advertise their establishments upon
the occasion of opening shop for the first time,
or after enlargement or repair. Advertisements are both printed and written, and

scarlet paper is the material usually employed. A brief summary of the contents of some of the most common may perhaps interest the reader, if he will again bear me company in imagination into a Chinese street. Here is one issued by a concern styling itself "a benefit to society," and which undertakes to prescribe gratis for those who are poor and feeble. A literal translation of its 458 characters would be scarcely expedient, although, in the matter of delicacy, the advertisement might compare favourably with many of a like kind found in newspapers in our own language. Suffice it to say that it conveys various pledges to attack with success, in an inconceivably brief space of time, all kinds of diseases, disgusting and otherwise, provided only the afflicted will swallow the drugs, pills, &c., dispensed by the concern. Here is another advertisement put forth by a druggist, who invites the public to swallow "pills manufactured out of a whole stag slaughtered with purity of purpose on a propitious day." Wealthy wholesale druggists not infrequently purchase large and handsome stags, which they expose in a pen at the

entrance of the shop, until a propitious day
can be selected for the animal's conversion into
medicine, when he is deliberately pounded
entire into a pulp, out of which pills are made.
These pills, it is believed, invigorate the system, and dispel any distemper or evil humour
which may be lurking in the tissues. Here
again is another placard by a quack. He
likewise styles himself a " world's benefactor,"
and he professes to be accessible only on the
even days of the month, and then only at eight
o'clock A.M.   Whether he gives this out in
order to enhance the idea of his professional
importance, or whether he devotes his odd
days and afternoons to other engagements,
does not appear.

Next comes the puff of a gentleman who
declares that he alone is conversant with the
true art of second sight, as practised by means
of the .circular mirror. This is a class of
persons to whom victims of petty thefts are in
the habit of applying in order to discover lost
property. One of these performers was once
called in by my servants, on the occasion
of a theft of some articles of clothing which
occurred on my own premises. After various

incantations and burnings of incense and joss-
paper in a dark room, he selected one out of
two or three little boys who happened to be
standing by, and placed him before a looking-
glass. The child was then asked if he observed
anything; on his replying in the negative,
another child was picked out and the same
process gone through. The little fellow peered
into the glass, and straightway declared he
saw something; and he then proceeded to tell
how he could distinguish a man dressed in
a white jacket and blue trowsers enter the
premises by such and such a door; how he
could see the thief pass along such and such
a passage, enter such and such a room, open
such and such a box, take out therefrom so
and so, make it up into a bundle, throw it
out of a window, and then creep away to
another part of the premises, and jump over
the wall into the road. The innocent and yet
earnest manner of the child, as he went
through these details, gave his story all the
weight of a supernatural revelation to the
wondering and credulous bystanders, and no
amount of banter on my part could succeed in
shaking their conviction that the process of

the theft had been correctly described, and that the perpetrators would be eventually traced out thereby. I must do the pretender the justice to state that he showed himself particularly anxious to persuade my own little boy, of seven years old, to act as medium, and would no doubt have employed him in that capacity, but that he stoutly objected to be made a tool of. An exactly similar method of divining by means of a child looking into a mirror or pool of water exists, it appears, amongst the modern Egyptians; and a very interesting description of the process may be found in Mr. E. W. Lane's work on the manners and customs of that people.

Our next advertisement is a playbill. It purports to be issued by a concern styling itself "Tea-garden of the Crimson *Olea fragrans.*" The name "tea-garden" is merely a blind to keep the advertiser clear of police exactions and interference, theatres being strictly prohibited by Chinese law, and actors being regarded as the very scum of society. Evasive and romantic designations are always given to theatres. Here is a playbill, emanating from a concern rejoicing in the name of

" Fragrance fills the Hall." Another is designated " The Garden of the Three Exquisites ;" and a fourth styles itself "The Chamber of the Yellow Olea." The " olea," only known in England as an exotic, is a highly-scented flower, much prized by the Chinese, and which consequently enters largely into their conceptions of the delicate and beautiful. Our particular playbill first suggests, in a persuasive tone, that rainy or windy weather should not be permitted to interfere with a punctual attendance. It then describes the plot of the piece that is to be represented, some episode in the life of a martial hero of the olden time. Such scraps of the ancient history of the country, rendered piquant by the insertion of comical and often indelicate passages in the story of the heroes and heroines, form favourite subjects for the drama in China ; and it is amusing to observe the breathless interest depicted on the countenances of the crowded audience as they watch the representation through its tedious progress towards *dénouement*.

The establishment thus advertised is one of several which Chinese speculators have opened in the foreign settlement of Shanghae with the assistance of foreign capital and under cover of foreign surroundings; but as a rule there are no buildings specially devoted to theatrical representations as with us. Companies of actors when formed travel about the country and engage themselves to committees of temples or guilds, or to wealthy individuals who may be festively inclined, for a week or a month at a time; and the representation usually takes place in a raised open pavilion with which every temple or club-house court is provided, and admission is given to the public gratis; no regular hours are kept, and the play is carried on with short intermissions for food and rest throughout the day and often nights, accompanied always by the incessant clanging of gongs and music of the most distracting character. Women are never seen on the stage, the female parts being taken by men who are educated to it from their childhood, and who imitate the feminine gait and voice to perfection.

One more advertisement is worthy of notice before we leave the subject. It is that of a lecturer, who undertakes to give readings out of the history of the Three Kingdoms, a chronicle of a favourite era in the Chinese history, which teems with martial and romantic incident. He likewise begs that " gentlemen will condescend to come early, and not be deterred by the inclemencies of the weather." Readings of this kind are generally given in tea-shops. They serve to collect custom for the establishment, whose host, no doubt, makes it worth the while of the lecturer to render his shop attractive, independently of any stray cash that may fall to the entertainer's share when the hat is sent round.

CHAPTER VIII.

MANDARIN YAMENS IN CHINA.

PROCEEDING along a Chinese street a stranger
would not fail to notice its intersection now
and again by a large palisaded enclosure, with
a huge ornamental gateway of three doors on
the one side, and a high blank wall facing the
gate on the other, the latter rudely daubed
with the picture of a rampant dragon in red
and white paint. This is the entrance court of
a *Yamen*, or the residence, as well as public
office of a mandarin; on either side, where
the street enters and leaves the enclosure, is
a roughly-constructed barrier gate, one surmounted by the characters "East office gate,"
the other by "West office gate." In the case
of a high-class *yamen*, such as that of a
viceroy, the thoroughfare is turned so as to
go round to the back of the front wall, and a
notice is stuck up to the effect that all officials
under a certain rank are to dismount from
their horses or leave their sedan-chairs at the

barrier gate. The main gate with the three doors is always placed so as to face towards the south, and where the street happens to run north and south, a cross street is opened, into which the *yamen* is made to face with east and west entrances on the two sides. Certain superstitious grounds, connected with the supposed position of the sun, give occasion to this arrangement, and even the Emperor himself, when sitting in state, has his face turned towards the south. The several barriers and other gateways of a *yamen* are usually surmounted with inscriptions which vary according to the functions and grade of the official, but are always couched in grandiloquent language. Those for instance placed over the gates of the Taotae's *yamen* at Shanghae are (translated into English), " Protector and administrator of twenty cities," and " Cleanser and purifier of three rivers," and these may be taken as a fair sample of all others throughout the country, the cherishing, protecting, improving, purifying, and beneficent characteristics ascribed to the incumbent within, being only too frequently in marked contrast to the reality, as far as the people

governed are concerned. The interiors of the
yamens consist of suites of rooms, arranged
after a stereotyped notion for the public and
private needs of the retainers, who are always
very numerous. Some few *yamens*, more especially those belonging to high-class officials,
are richly-decorated, well-constructed buildings, but, as a rule, they do not bear looking
into; and they are generally maintained in a
wretched condition of unrepair, as no mandarin is understood to hold the same office
for a longer term than three years, and he
has of course no interest in expending money
upon his temporary domicile or offices during
that period.

Observe now the procession emerging from
the *yamen*. At the head of the ragamuffin
crew appear two or four lictors dressed in tall
black felt hats, and armed with whips with
which they are supposed to flog the people
into reverential submission, whilst the great
man passes by. The tall hats and whips of
these rascals (for rascals they invariably are,
having to live by their wits, poor creatures)
may be seen hanging up at the gates of most
yamens, ominous of what those who are unfor-

tunate enough to get dragged into the inner
precincts may expect. After the lictors come
a group of boys bearing red boards inscribed
with gilt characters. Some of these give the
several ranks and titles of the mandarin;
others convey commands to be silent, to stand
back, &c. Then comes the umbrella inscribed
with the ten thousand names, a proof of popularity which every mandarin covets, and after
that the sedan-chair, borne by four or more
bearers, according to the rank of the official
within. Military mandarins ride on horses
or mules, it being considered effeminate and
unsoldierlike to sit at ease in a sedan-chair.
After the dignitary himself, follow the secretaries, card-bearer, personal servants, &c., all
carried likewise in sedans, but of the most
sorry description and having only two bearers
each. The sedans used by the mandarins are
always covered with broadcloth, the colour of
which is defined according to the rank, and
they are handsomely lined and fitted within,
sometimes with expensive furs. In Peking
and the northernmost Provinces, two-wheeled
carts without springs are used instead of
sedans.

The general impression out of China is that
a mandarin spends his .days in idleness and
luxury, whilst he battens .upon the booty
wrung by himself and followers from the
unhappy people over whom he is placed;
but this is not altogether a correct view.
Although little can be said for the general
results of mandarin administration in the
way of promoting the best interests of the
population, and although the wretched pit-
tances allowed by the government as salaries
lead to a vast amount of peculation and
rapacity, yet the Chinese officials as a class
lead a laborious life, and instances are not
wanting of individuals winning the esteem
and even devotion of the people. Owing to
the peculiar system of administration, duties,
which, according to our Western ideas, are
best distributed amongst a number of officials
and departments, are in China concentred in
one individual, and what with judicial business
both civil and criminal, finance, police, transport, commissariat, and a number of other
heterogeneous duties, a mandarin of any
standing always has his hands perfectly full.
Office hours commence with the dawn and

often only close with the cessation of demands
upon the attention which evening of necessity
brings. Nor may an official hope for any
relief in the diversion which society affords.
A mandarin is not expected to have any
friendships or intimacies outside of his *yamen*,
and he cannot encourage visitors or loiterers
within its precincts without laying himself
open to a charge of favoritism or corruption.
He may not even go out of his *yamen* openly
for exercise or recreation. As a rule his
secretaries are all-powerful, and in cases where
any venality is practised it is always accomplished by or through these men. A *yamen*
is in fact practically closed to the public, save
through the good offices of a secretary or some
other of the numerous underlings who continually haunt its gates and courts. Consequently a mandarin with the best intentions
may, even without his privity, become a curse
to his neighbourhood.

I can myself vouch for an instance in which
an opium merchant, who had decamped after
a large transaction in opium, for which he
paid in spurious paper, actually took refuge
in the Taotae's *yamen*, and successfully con-

cealed himself there for weeks, although the Taotae and Consul together employed every appliance in their power for his capture, and large rewards were offered for his detection. He no doubt concluded his safest place was under the very roof of the court whose warrants had been issued for his apprehension; and as far as the mandarin was concerned I had no reason to imagine but that he acted *bonâ fide* all the while.

It has been remarked that instances are not unfrequent in which the purity and patriotism of a mandarin receive appreciation at the hands of the people. A common method of expressing it is by the presentation of the umbrella alluded to in connection with the mandarin cavalcade. Foreigners call this article an "umbrella," but it partakes more of the nature of a circular canopy, being carried on a staff in front of the mandarin when he goes abroad, and held aloft over his head whenever he alights from his sedan. It is made of scarlet silk, and on the deep borders which encircle it are embroidered in yellow or black silk the names of the donors.

At other times tablets bearing complimentary inscriptions are given as testimonials, and these are much prized by the recipients, and used to decorate their best receiving rooms. Another and more comical method of exhibiting the public estimation of official probity and worth is for a deputation of the inhabitants to wait upon a mandarin at one of the gates of the city at the moment of his making his farewell exit, and to beg the gift of his boots, which are thenceforward reverently cherished in some temple as public property. Chinese populations are equally ready at expressing their disapprobation of the conduct of their public men when it happens to obtrude itself prominently upon their notice, or when they become the victims to its consequences. Lampoons are a favourite channel for denunciation; and not unfrequently the popular indignation is evinced by a positive onslaught upon the unfortunate functionary, either in his *yamen* or when he ventures into the streets. On such occasions he is certain to be reprimanded by his superiors for inability to conciliate and restrain his people, or to be transferred to another sphere of duty.

CHAPTER IX.

OPIUM SMOKING.

NEARLY every stranger who visits a Chinese city considers his round of sight-seeing incomplete until he has witnessed the process of opium smoking. The dens in which the drug is doled out to its victims, although numerous enough in every city, are not easily distinguishable, its vendors not having yet got over the fear of penal consequences, which, until the import and sale of opium were legalized, always attended any connection with the traffic. The vice, therefore, has not the concomitants of glitter and gewgaw to assist in attracting its victims, which are found associated with the similar bane of drinking in our own country. The reader will, perhaps, be interested in visiting in imagination one of these establishments, and observing for himself what is to be seen therein. Although situated in a main thoroughfare with pretentious shops and buildings on either hand, the opium den is usually remarkable for the mean filthy front

which it presents to the street, and the only
sign or mark which betokens its existence to
the uninitiated is a diminutive dirty paper-
lantern over the doorway, bearing the inscription " As you like it," or sometimes the
announcement " Foreign earth " is ventured
upon in small characters upon a card stuck in
a window. A step further over the threshold
reveals a dilapidated paper screen or two,
placed athwart the room so as to cut off the
interior, as far as possible, from outer observation. On the other side of these screens, in
a murky dark atmosphere, lie the smokers
stretched upon a dozen wretched platforms, in
all stages of indulgence, whilst two or three
foul ragged attendants stoop in corners over
pans of the seething mixture preparing it for
consumption. When ready for use it has the
appearance of treacle, and is of the consistency
of melting india-rubber. In this condition it
is presented to the smoker, who with the end
of a silver skewer twists up a small quantity
about the size of a pea, which he places in the
minute aperture on the top of his pipe bowl,
and then, holding it to the flame of the lamp,
he sucks up the fumes.

Travellers are too apt, when treating of opium smoking amongst the Chinese, to convey the impression that it is employed in the same way as tobacco. Nothing can be more different than the two processes of smoking. In the case of the drug, the fumes are inhaled into the lungs, and such portion of them as is rejected passes out of the nostrils. After long habit some smokers manage to inhale the greater part of the fumes. The pipe used, moreover, is but of one kind, and it could not be employed in smoking tobacco, the aperture at the top of the bowl being only large enough to admit a good-sized pin.

The effect upon the individual, when indulged in habitually and to excess, is certainly debasing, and there is, perhaps, no vicious habit from which complete recovery is more difficult. At the same time I would caution the reader against an unqualified acceptance of the tales of horror one hears and reads of in connection with opium smoking in China. How that, for instance, every fifth, or tenth, or twentieth, or even fortieth man in the empire is a victim to the habit; how that the opium hells are as abundant as the provision shops, and crowded day and night with hundreds of infatuated wretches hurrying to their ruin; how that skeletons haunt the streets, and whole families, beggared by drugged husbands and fathers, may be seen dying in the highways and fields; and so on. There are opium dens no doubt, and quite numerous enough to sadden the philanthropic observer, and the victims which the drug drags to misery and death are also, alas! beyond all counting. But what is the vice, or where the country, of which the same may not be said with equal or approximate truth. Indeed, were I asked to state candidly in which part of the world I thought the effects of vicious indulgence are more outwardly observable, socially speaking, I certainly should not name China. Statistics on the subject cannot be relied on. It is known to a chest how much Indian-grown drug is imported into the country, but there is no means of estimating the quantity of native opium produced, and I do not believe that there is any person sufficiently informed on the subject to be able to state, with any approach to accuracy, what proportion the smokers of the drug bear to the general population. The most that can be asserted with truth, is that the vice is a general one, more especially prevalent in districts near the sea-coast and great commercial centres, that a considerable proportion of its victims indulge to an excess ruinous to health and prospects, and that it has been gaining ground upon the people with rapid strides during the past few years. It is, at any rate, a matter of congratulation that a Chinaman confines his indulgence to opium smoking, and that drink does not add to the vicious chains by which he is enslaved. A ray of hope, too, for the Chinese may be found in the fact, which I have before stated, that the indigenous cultivation of the drug is gaining ground, for the material being much inferior to that imported from India, it is just possible that the depreciation may have the effect in the end of decreasing the taste for the article, or that the more general use of it that must ensue may rouse the public to a more earnest sense of the ruinous results attending its indulgence, and, as a consequence, to a determined effort of resistance to its seductive influences.

CHAPTER X.

INFANTICIDE.

THE Chinese have the credit amongst most Englishmen of being a nation of Infanticides, and the impression is to be attributed to the stories which cursory visitors, and even observing travellers, are apt to bring home. These will tell, it may be, of " baby towers," standing in the vicinity of most towns, and of suspicious little bundles noticed in pools and canals; of carts, which are said to go round for the purpose of collecting castaway children ; of miniature coffins strewed about the fields, &c. Such things have no doubt intruded themselves upon the notice, but the observers have not taken the trouble, or, perhaps, from ignorance of the language, have not always found themselves able to inquire, how or why these remains came to be so disposed of. Had they done so, they would have learnt that the relics seen were by no means in every instance, or even nearly so, those of castaway or murdered infants, the Chinese being one of those people who do not consider it essential to give formal sepulture to a child under a certain age. The truth in this, as in most other cases, may be discovered to lie between the two extremes. There are towns and districts where infanticide is practised, in some to an infamous extent, in others to a less degree ; there are others again where it is not known at all as a habit, and in the majority of cities I am inclined to believe that it is a crime no more indulged in than is the case in some European towns, and then only with the object of concealing another act of frailty. If there is any distinction to be made, it is in favour of the northern and midland, as against the southern and coast provinces.

But as a rule one has only to enter a Chinese city or hamlet to be convinced that the stories about infanticide must, to say the least, have been exaggerated, for the swarms of children of both sexes which lounge about the doors and infest the gutters is something remarkable. The Chinese, moreover, exhibit a marked attachment for their offspring. At

every few steps in a Chinese street may be
encountered a delighted father, or a decrepit
grandame, proudly fondling a chubby child,
dressed in all the colours of the rainbow, and
loaded with as many amulets, charms, and
ornaments as it can well carry. It is a common practice to adorn infant caps and hoods
with texts, in gold and silver-gilt letters,
expressive of good wishes for the wearer's
health and welfare. A very favourite motto
of this kind is "Long life, wealth, and
honour;" another also much used is, "A safe
passage through all critical periods and obnoxious influences." Very often a row of
little gilt idols decorates the frontlet, to represent the eight genii, a Taouist fancy; or the
eighteen saints, a Buddhist superstition; the
idea in either case being to record the wish
that the childish wearer may, like the legendary individuals represented, pass safely
through all the ills of its mortal life to a
similar fruition of afterglory and beatitude.

Boys are very naturally more highly prized
than girls, but I have never observed the one
more lovingly cherished than the other where
there are a number of both in one family.

Boys, however, enjoy the advantage of education, which the Chinese do not seem to consider essential for girls. Women are consequently seldom found able to read. Instances do occur in which daughters of wealthy families are educated simultaneously with the sons, but these are unhappily exceptional, dress and self-adornment, and sometimes music,* being regarded as the proper amusements of the Chinese lady.

The practice of selling children is nevertheless tolerated, and it has become very prevalent of late years, owing no doubt to the vast amount of poverty and wretchedness which everywhere prevails. Scarcely a year passes but some part of the country is devastated by a flood or drought, and, the population being principally agricultural, the amount of misery occasioned is always immense. The Supreme Government and local executives at such conjunctures profess great concern for the sufferings of the people, and measures are set on foot at times on an extensive scale to organize schemes for relief, but inefficiency and corruption nearly always interfere to defeat the

* See Appendix.

most beneficent intentions, and little or nothing is eventually effected beyond the bestowal by Imperial favour of a new tablet upon a River God, or the offering of a special sacrifice to propitiate some deity supposed to be offended.

The extensive rebellions which are perpetually occurring are another fertile source of impoverishment to the country. The Taeping insurrection was, perhaps, the most fearful scourge of this kind which ever fell upon the unhappy people of China, and although years have passed since it was quelled, the sad effects of it are still everywhere visible in Provinces which were once the richest and most thickly populated in China. I have often traversed the 250 miles of country lying between Hangchow and Nanking, and of which the Grand Canal and its numerous affluents are the principal arteries, and I can conceive of no more melancholy sight than the acres of ground that one passes through strewn with remains of once thriving cities, and the miles upon miles of rich land, once carefully parcelled off indeed into fields and gardens, but now only growing long coarse grass and brambles, the home of the pheasant, the deer, and the wild pig. It is not to be wondered at then that children should be a burden upon millions of poverty-stricken parents, and that even infanticide should present a welcome relief from inevitable wretchedness.

Although it must be admitted that children are thus bought and sold in China, the slavery which ensues is attended with but an infinitesimal share of the evils which mark the institution in other countries. Boys are purchased for adoption into families as sons or sons-in-law, and not unfrequently to be brought up as play-actors. Girls are sought for as domestic servants in families, as well as for purposes of prostitution. In neither case is the slavery perpetual, and it is only where the girls are consigned to the public markets that their fate is to be deplored. Even then, if they possess any attractions, or are fortunate enough to be accomplished (for a classical and musical education is frequently accorded to members of this unhappy class), they often have the good fortune to be selected by wealthy men as wives, and so end their days in respectability and comfort. Girls who are bought into

families as domestics constantly marry into
the family, or an equally suitable settlement
is eventually found for them by their proprietors elsewhere.

CHAPTER XI.

EATING AND DRINKING IN CHINA.

ANOTHER fallacy which prevails in regard
to the Chinese, is that their food consists of
dogs, cats, rats, and other garbage, and I have
sometimes even been asked by persons, otherwise well informed, whether foreign residents
in China are not unfortunate enough to find
themselves restricted to the same diet. This
impression has, no doubt, got abroad from the
fact that early travellers have observed puppies
and kittens exposed for sale in the markets of
Canton amongst articles for table consumption, and have been led to infer too hastily,
perhaps, that these animals are vended for
food, whereas they are thus sold for domestic
uses almost exclusively. I will not assert
that dogs and cats are never eaten; for there
are poor, more particularly in the south, who
do not object to dine off a plump rodent when
they can procure nothing better, and there
are actually restaurants, in Canton especially,

devoted to the preparation of canine dishes, for the delectation of a particular class of gourmands to be found in that city. There are always strong suspicions, moreover, cherished by foreign residents, who are unlucky enough to lose their pet dogs, that these have been purloined in view of their goodly condition, it being the Chinese idea that we foreigners feed our canine pets upon the best of mutton ; and as a proof that Chinese are to be found whose appetites are not of the most fastidious, I myself once saw a mob of boat-people fight for the carcases of some horses which our military had caused to be shot on the river-side by reason of their being affected with glanders.

Notwithstanding these facts, I must nevertheless maintain that the Chinese as a race are not foul feeders. The truth is, that, unless a Chinaman is at all well to do, he rarely indulges in a meat meal at all, the usual food for the masses being, in the midland and southern provinces, plain boiled rice, with a relish of pickled fish or vegetables, salted eggs, a curd made of lentils, &c. When meat can be afforded, pork is always the favourite dish, and amongst the higher classes the bill

H

of fare is varied by the addition of mutton, poultry, venison, or game. Sundry delicacies are also introduced, which are almost unknown to European palates, such as bêche-de-mer, sea-weed, shark's-fin, jelly fish, the edible bird's-nest, ducks' tongues, pigeons' and plovers' eggs, &c. Some of these can be recommended as well worthy of introduction to our own tables, where possibly they might be rendered even more toothsome by the science and experience which European artists could bring to bear upon their cooking qualities. There is a soup common to first-class dinners in China, composed of shark's-fin, bird's-nest, and sea slug, with pigeons' or plovers' eggs floating entire on its surface, which I consider quite equal, if not superior, to any of our richest soups, excepting perhaps turtle. The great objection to a Chinese dinner is its wearisome length, from the large number of courses of which it is usually composed. The dishes, too, are apt to be rich and greasy.

It has been observed that drunkenness is not a Chinese failing: on the contrary, I am happy to be able to bear witness that John Chinaman is a most temperate creature.

During the whole course of my many years' residence in the country I do not remember to have seen a dozen instances of actual drunkenness. They do imbibe spirituous liquors manufactured out of rice and other cereals, but it is only occasionally at family gatherings, periodical festivals, friendly dinners, and such like occasions, and then they seldom get beyond flushed faces, and cheerful clamour. They seldom seem to take to drink as a habit. There are exceptions of course, but these are rare. A public-house is an institution unknown. Weak tepid tea without the admixture of milk or sugar is the prevailing beverage of all classes, and teapots are placed within reach everywhere to gratify this habit at frequent intervals during the day. This is especially observable amongst mechanics, with whom, be the circumstances what they may, the teapot may be seen as a never-failing companion.

Open tea-houses, somewhat on the principle of the continental restaurant, abound in every street and public garden, and these are frequented not only by the thirsty passers-by, but by persons wishing to have a half-hour's friendly or business chat. In some of these public readers or lecturers may be found, for the attraction or amusement of customers. In the summer months wealthy folk cause huge pans of ready-made tea to be placed at the corners of streets or in crowded thorough-fares, for the convenience of the poor; very much as permanent drinking-fountains are now erected in our cities.

CHAPTER XII.

CHINESE SOCIAL INSTITUTIONS.

ALTHOUGH, as has been stated in a previous chapter, there is no such thing as social intercourse between the Chinese and foreigners, it cannot fail to strike even a cursory observer that they are a sociable people amongst themselves, and that their courtesies are of a most laboured and punctilious character. Visiting, for example, is a serious affair, and has to be conducted in accordance with a conventional code, which prescribes all kinds of formalities varying with the respective positions of the visitor and visited. Cards are extensively used, but of a colour and style far different from what we are accustomed to employ as mediums in the interchange of civilities. The shapes and sizes, moreover, vary considerably with the occasion and the individual. The common plain card used between equals consists of a single sheet of crimson paper about 12 inches long by 4 inches broad, with the surname and name stamped or written in black ink, the more mammoth-like the character the more imposing and respectable. This is generally used amongst officials pretending to some rank or position. A card of about half the size is used by men of inferior rank and commoners, or even by the higher officials where the parties are on intimate terms. Then there is the "complete card," as it is called, which is only employed on grand occasions, such as new year calls, visits of congratulation on weddings, births, birthdays, acquirement of literary degrees, and the like, also of condolence on deaths, &c. This card is folded, and must contain ten folds, each sheet of which is as large as that of the first card described. The name of the individual is inscribed on the right hand lower corner of the first fold, prefixed by the words, " Your stupid younger brother," and followed by the compliment, " bows his head and pays his respects." When the person visited belongs to a generation senior to the visitors, the latter styles himself, " Your stupid nephew," if to two generations senior, the visitor writes, " Your more than stupid nephew." Should the individual visited belong to a younger generation, the visitor takes to himself the name of "uncle" instead of "nephew," retaining, however, the depreciatory appellative of "stupid." There are still further varieties of self-designation, according to the particular gradations of relationship, but those I have quoted will suffice to give an idea of the punctilious rules peculiar to Chinese visiting; I may add that the card last described is, as a matter of etiquette, always understood to be returned to the visitor; it being, presumably, expensive to leave such voluminous proofs of regard with a number of friends.

I have often been asked by inquisitive people in England to say "How d'ye do " or "Good morning" in Chinese, and have been all but put down as an impostor because I was unable to comply with the requisition. The fact is the Chinese make use of neither expression when they meet. A bow, with the mute folding of the hands together, is the usual mark of recognition when friends encounter each other on common occasions, and if anything is said it is "Tsing, Tsing," meaning, "I pray you, I pray you," which has been barbarized by us into "Chinchin."

The intention is on either part to entreat the other to take the precedence, and much time is lost, when visiting, in a friendly antagonism between host and guest as to which should first take a seat, or lift a cup of tea, or touch the proffered dish. Inattention to this formality is regarded as a discourtesy, and would stamp the offender as a boor, unacquainted with the commonest rules of polite society. Many and many a time have I been rendered very uncomfortable, when visiting Chinese officials in the company of naval officers and others, who chanced to be ignorant of this peculiarity in Chinese customs, by observing the disgust depicted on the mandarins' countenances at seeing their visitors straightway take possession of the seats offered, without making the slightest deprecatory gesture, or waiting until the host could find his own proper seat. Of course nothing was further from the intention of my friends than to offend a prejudice, but I fear the effect was none the less to confirm the preconceived opinion on the part of the Chinaman that barbarism was after all essential to the foreign nature.

Apropos of visiting and cards, and as illustrative of Chinese customs, I may here allude to a most singular circumstance connected with a card which I once received in China. It was from a lady, intimating her intention to commit suicide at a specified date. She was very young and attractive, and belonged to a wealthy family. Unfortunately, the Chinese gentleman, to whom she had been affianced from childhood, had died just before the date fixed upon for their nuptials, and she gave out that she deemed it her duty to render her widowhood irrevocable by dying with her betrothed. So she sent cards round to the neighbouring gentry, giving notice of the purpose I have mentioned. No attempt was made by her relatives or by the local authorities to frustrate the insane design, the general opinion, on the contrary, being that she was about to perform a meritorious act. I even went so far as to appeal to the mandarins to put a stop to the proceeding, but they assured me that interference on their part might lead to a popular demonstration. Eventually, on the day named, the woman did deliberately sacrifice her life in the presence of thousands. A stage was erected in

the open fields, with a tented frame over it,
from which was suspended a slip of scarlet
crape; one end of this she adjusted round her
neck. She then embraced a little boy, probably a little brother, presented by a person
standing by, and having let fall a veil over
her face, she mounted a chair and resolutely
jumped off it, her little clasped hands saluting
the assemblage as her fast-failing frame twirled
round with the tightening cord.

As far as I could ascertain the woman was
not drugged, neither was she hounded on to
her fate by a fanatic mob, as was, I believe,
the practice at Suttees in India, but the im-
molation was entirely a voluntary act on her
part. I confess I could not muster courage
to be present, but some friends who were
staying with me witnessed the proceeding,
and they all concurred in declaring it to have
been one of the most affecting sights that they
had seen. Sacrifices of this kind are not uncommon in certain districts, but they are not
always performed in public and with so much
of *éclat*.

Friendly and family gatherings are constantly going on, and there is nothing that a

Chinaman or woman loves so well as a gossip over a pipe and a cup of tea. A favourite pastime is for literary men to meet at a fashionable restaurant or at some romantic retreat amongst sylvan scenery, and indulge a friendly antagonism in the composition of rhymes, one against the other, draughts of wine being the forfeit incurred by the least successful.

Their women do not mix in society, but their social influence is by no means limited, and the older ladies in families especially are looked up to and treated with much deference and consideration. Although confined very much to the house, they appear to be happy enough in each other's companionship, if one may judge by the merriment always to be heard going on in what are termed "the inner apartments." Amongst shopkeepers, mechanics, agriculturists, and the lower classes generally, the women of necessity occupy a more prominent position in the household, and are consequently to be seen mixing more freely with the men, and taking their full share of the daily labour.

Marriage ceremonies are conducted with

much formality, the rules for which vary according to the rank and means of the parties, and the particular province or district in which they reside. The pledging by the couple of each other in wine, and their united act of obeisance to their several parents if alive, or to their *manes* if deceased, appear to constitute the really binding process in all cases. No official registration nor religious rite is considered necessary, the contract being strictly a civil one. The tie is held indissoluble and sacred as a rule, but instances occur in which a husband considers himself entitled to put away his wife, and public opinion sustains him in the proceeding. The grounds of divorce are some seven in number, and one or two of them would be regarded by us as puerile to a degree, as for instance a persistent habit of loquacity on the part of the lady. On the other hand, there are certain circumstances in which divorce is not permitted under any consideration. A man, for example, who by some freak of fortune attains to wealth or honour in after-life may not repudiate the partner of his poorer years. Polygamy is common amongst the well-to-do, but rather in the shape of concubinage, the wife *par excellence* always maintaining her position and rights *quoad* the rest of the household; her children likewise taking precedence of those of the other wives. Early marriage is universal, and such a thing as an old maid or bachelor is entirely unknown. But it is not considered respectable for a widow to marry again, and, where a betrothed girl loses her affianced husband, it is regarded as extremely meritorious for her to abjure the wedded state altogether. So marked is public opinion in this particular, that testimonials are often voted by the people to commemorate such instances of fidelity.

Prostitution exists in all the large cities, but the law and public opinion combine to keep it under a certain check, and the practice of early marriage must have a salutary effect in counteracting its baneful influences.

Matrimonial alliances between persons of the same surname are not tolerated, it being presumed that they must of necessity be related. Consequently, cousins by the father's side may not interwed, although those by the mother's side are permitted to do so. This is perhaps as much a sentimental as a legal objection, and it is to be ascribed to the patriarchal system, which has always prevailed in China, of members of the same family or clan congregating together in the same locality. This has been so universally the practice for ages past, that whole villages may be found nowadays with inhabitants all bearing the same patronymic, and according a deference little short of loyalty to the aged leaders of the clan. Yet, strange to say, the list of family surnames distributed amongst the hundreds of millions who crowd the country number little over four hundred, so that the selection for matrimonial purposes is exceedingly limited as far as the similarity of surname is concerned. Nevertheless, the restriction does not appear to be found irksome.

CHAPTER XIII.

CORRESPONDENCE AND THE PRESS.

CORRESPONDENCE by letter is very general in China, the post being conveyed between city and city by couriers, who earn their livelihood by carrying letters at a certain rate of mileage, agreed upon by general consent. Official communications are dispatched to and fro by special messengers, who, in cases ,of emergency, have horses provided for them, and so attain a speed of 150 to 170 miles *per diem*. Carrier-pigeons, too, are largely employed by business houses. Governmental post-offices and stamps are as yet a dream of the future. Business letters are written upon plain white paper, and folded very much as ours used to be thirty or forty years ago, before envelopes came into vogue. No sealing-wax is used, but the fold is fastened down by means of a little paste, and a seal bearing a private monogram, or some lucky motto, is affixed to the suture with colouring matter.

Friendly notes and billets are inscribed upon slips of delicately tinted paper, tastefully embossed with flowers, vases, and sundry quaint devices peculiar to the Chinese, and these are enclosed in decorated envelopes, a convenience, by the way, which the Chinese introduced long before it was thought of in the West. The mammoth cards previously described are also used for scribbling notes on. The language is always as flowery as the material, and special care is taken to employ the most euphemistic expressions possible, when referring to the individual addressed, and the most depreciatory when alluding to the writer or to his belongings.

Curiously enough signatures have not that importance attached to them by the Chinese which they possess in most countries and amongst people of business habits. A commonplace letter is not closed with anything like our conventional " Yours obediently," or "faithfully," or "sincerely," or "affectionately," followed by the sign manual of the writer; but it ends with the subscription, " written on

such and such a lucky day by younger brother
so and so." And where the identity of the
writer is a matter of moment, a small seal
containing a monogram of the name or of
some favourite motto is impressed upon the
spot covered by the date or the name. The
only approach to a signature used by the
Chinese is a device embodying two or three
characters in one, and written so rapidly as to
be beyond the possibility of counterfeit. This
conceit is mostly affected by literary men.
Promissory notes, bills, receipts, agreements,
and such like are authenticated by a stamp,
bearing, not the name of the concern, but the
style or appellation by which it is known in
business.

In official communications the Chinese indulge the identical weakness that we have for
the use of awe-inspiring stationery, although
perhaps they exaggerate it to a more formidable extent. I have seen, for instance, an
official letter in folds measuring together some
forty feet in length and enclosed in an en-
velope 24 inches by 10. A book might be
written describing all the various forms of
letters and styles of address which official

I

etiquette prescribes to the several ranks and departments of mandarindom. As a rule the communications do credit to the scholarship of the writers as well as to the penmanship of the secretaries. As in the case of common letters, no signature is ever attached, the official seal being the sole mark of authentication.

The Chinese cherish a curious veneration for all written paper. A scribbler who does not care to retain the scrap he has been writing on will not be seen to tear it up into bits to be thrown heedlessly away. He will carefully crunch it up, and either put the ball into the first fire he may come across, or he will pocket it until he finds a basket, which he is sure to discover somewhere close by, placed for the purpose, and the contents of which are scrupulously burnt. Such receptacles may be noticed here and there in the streets, and devout persons frequently place urns covered in by miniature temples on the wayside, for the reception and decent disposal of written or printed scraps, with the inscription over the tiny doorway, "Respect and treat kindly inscribed paper." There are also certain people, who, by way of performing a meritorious act, hire collectors to go round a town with baskets, and, on receiving their gleanings, heap these together on a sacred bonfire.

The Press, which holds so important a position in this and other Western countries, can hardly be said to be even known in China. One paper alone is in general circulation, a sort of official gazette, which professes to publish the principal memorials of high functionaries to the Emperor, the Imperial decrees and rescripts, and lists of changes in official circles. It is said to be printed in Peking, from wax blocks, and is distributed thence by postal couriers to all the Government offices in the provinces, whence transcripts get abroad amongst the common people. It contains no original matter of any kind, and, curiously enough, like the earliest newspaper issues in our own country, it is not in any way used as an advertising medium. Public opinion finds no expression in its pages, save through the State papers which it contains, and some of which, it must be confessed, are not wanting in outspoken criticism, both of departments and individuals, and at times even of the Imperial Court itself. In this

respect at any rate it may be said to be far in
advance of our own early London Gazettes,
which never contained any intelligence that it
did not suit the purposes of the Court to publish.
It is at the same time a fact worthy of notice,
that the country in which the art of printing
was earliest known, and in which literature
has had an undoubted and influential sway
for many centuries, should at 'this moment be
the only one amongst nations making any
pretence to civilization, in which the press
has no footing as a vehicle of opinion.   The
fact is the more remarkable, since the Chinese
are essentially a reading people, and show
their appreciation of newspapers by the
avidity with which the two or three native
papers issued by the Shanghae foreign presses
are read, and by the eagerness with which
they seek to have the articles in English
papers translated for their information.   It is
my conviction that there is nothing that would
tend more surely and speedily to open the eyes
of the Chinese Government and people to a true
sense of the advantages of Western commerce,
progress, and civilization, and prepare the
way for more extended and friendly relations

with foreigners, than a few well-conducted newspapers in the native language, and no channel for effecting the change would prove more acceptable to the people themselves. Much credit is due to the partial attempts which have already been made in this direction at Shanghae, but the publications turned out are still sadly lacking in the composition and style which are needed to ensure general acceptance with the reading public.

CHAPTER XIV.

MODES OF SEPULTURE.

THE neighbourhood of a Chinese city is always remarkable for the vast number of tombs which meet the eye in every direction. Wherever there is a hill or elevation in a populous district it is certain to be thickly covered with earthen mounds, so thickly indeed that one wonders where any future dead will find room to lie; where the country is flat, mounds and coffins may be seen scattered about the fields, but as a rule a Chinaman prefers to lay his bones upon a slope. The grave when planted on a hill-side is always placed so as to cause the headstone to face down-hill, it being considered lucky for the remains to have a good position with respect to the " Feng Shuy," or geomantic influences of the locality. Wealthy people spend months and years in the selection of such a favourable spot, and grudge no outlay in securing it when found. Whether the remains receive all the benefit

intended may be a question, but such taste is
always exhibited in the selection of a point
from which the vista of hill and dale may be
seen to the best advantage, that some of the
most lovely and romantic views in China
may be had by climbing to first-class tombs
upon the hill-sides.

The Chinese modes of sepulture are various.
Wealthy families purchase plots of ground,
which they enclose and plant with pine, firs,
cypress, and other evergreens, and furnish
with temples, in which the ancestral tablets
are preserved, and the periodical sacrifices to
the *manes* of the departed performed. These
burial-places are reverently cherished for
generations, and are often most picturesque
and romantic spots. The tomb is generally
composed of one or more chambers constructed of brick, laid with mortar so peculiarly prepared with the admixture of rice
and sugar as to harden into a marble, and
defy the ravages of centuries. Over this is
placed a respectable mound, either covered with
plain sod and surmounted by some umbra-
geous evergreen, or cased with mortar. This
mound is encircled, except in front, by a low

substantial wall, which turns off to either side
at the entrance, and so describes as near as
possible the form of the Greek letter *omega*.
Fronting the entrance is the headstone, which
always bears a plain inscription, of which the
following is a fair translated specimen, " The
tomb of A. B., of Ningpo, of the reign of
Tungchih, of the Tatsing Dynasty; erected
on a propitious day in a vernal month of such
and such a year." The age, condition, or
history of the deceased is never given ; neither
do the inscriptions ever indulge in the eulo-
gistic comments or pathetic quotations so
common to epitaphs in Western countries.
In cases where the deceased was a person of
eminence, or a high public functionary, it is
customary to front the grave with an avenue
formed of several pairs of gigantic stone
figures of men and animals, which, although
but rude specimens of works of art, always combine to give the scene an imposing and solemn
character. This must, however, have been a
practice more common in ancient times than
now, for I cannot remember ever having observed any such monuments about the country
but what were hoary and ruinous with age. The

ancestor of the family and his spouse always occupy the most commanding spot in the enclosure facing the supposed " Feng Shuy," and the other branches of the family are assigned places on either side, the graves advancing towards the main gate as the generations descend.   I have seen them arranged in one or two instances with all the order and exactitude of a genealogical tree.

The middle and poorer classes are content to inter their dead upon the open hill side, sometimes erecting a brick or stone tomb, as above described over the remains, and sometimes only a plain earth mound.   In the plains a not uncommon method of burial is to place the coffin upon a stand a foot or two above the ground, and to construct over it a brick and mortar casing covered with a tiled roof, or, where the parties are very poor, a thatch or straw covering.   In the former case the brick walls may often be observed perforated with apertures in the shape of characters, with suitable meanings, such as, " Happiness," " Longevity,"   " Rest,"   " Beautiful   City," " Last   abode," and   such   like.   Children's remains,   as   has   already   been   stated,   the

Chinese do not consider it necessary to afford
sepulture to.   If those of mere infants, they
are tied up in matting and deposited in a lone
place, or thrown into a canal or general receptacle for infant dead.   When the children
are a little more advanced in years they are
placed in roughly constructed coffins, which
are laid down in any convenient solitary spot.
A walk round the walls of a Chinese city will
afford the opportunity of observing many
such a melancholy relic.

Public cemeteries may often be seen outside
the limits of a populous town, but these are
the properties of guilds or clubs instituted by
strangers resorting to said town for purposes
of business or otherwise.   The Chinese are a
very clannish people, and when a number of
persons belonging to the same province or
city find themselves congregated in a distant
locality they invariably set up a club, under
the direction of a committee selected annually
from amongst its most influential members.
The institution serves the double purpose of
an 'assembly room, where the clansmen can
discuss public questions or hold high festival,
and a court of arbitration to which they can

refer business disputes in preference to appearing before the local authorities. One of the
duties such an establishment undertakes is to
inter at the public expense the remains of any
poor members, and hence the necessity of a
cemetery for the purpose. Most of these cemeteries are furnished with a sacrificial temple,
to which are attached extensive suites of rooms
for the reception of the coffins of the richer
members, pending transmission home to their
own native districts; for a Chinaman prizes
beyond all things the privilege of laying his
bones near those of his forefathers. It is in
such receptacles for the dead that one can contemplate that curiosity, a Chinese coffin, in its
perfection. It is seldom decorated save with
the figure of the god of longevity, or with the
character meaning "length of years" carved
at either end. The quality and ponderosity
of the wood are the main points looked to, and
immense sums are expended, sometimes even
before death, in securing enormous blocks of
the most desirable material procurable. The
lid is morticed on, not screwed or nailed, and
the utmost care is taken to cement all joints,
so as not to leave the slightest crevice through

which air can enter or escape; a small aperture is, however, purposely drilled through that part of the lid which covers the face of the occupant, so as to leave a channel of exit and entrance for the spirit at its option. The precautions thus taken are so effectual, that one may wander all over such an establishment without perceiving any odour of decaying animal matter.

A Chinese is bound by custom and duty to repair and sacrifice at the graves of his deceased relatives on a certain day during the spring of each year, and it is both an interesting and curious sight to see the hill-sides on that and several succeeding days covered with parties of people dressed in white or sackcloth attending to this duty. It consists in " sweeping and sacrificing " as it is called, but actually weeding and repairing the precincts of the grave, and then burning a due quantity of paper money specially constructed for currency in the upper regions. Sometimes offerings of meat, fruit, cakes, and liquor, are presented. By some of the sacrificers the process is gone through as a true labour of love, and more respect and grief could not be exhibited were

the loss one but of a few days instead of years
old. But the majority perform the duty with
but small show of reverence or sorrow. In fact
the demeanour of the Chinese in respect to
their dead is often very contradictory. Women
will wail over a dead body in the house, and
even the men will blubber at one moment, and
at another they will be feasting, chatting, and
cracking jokes together, as if nothing had
happened. A coffin will be allowed to lie under
a shed for months or out in the fields with but
a scanty covering of thatch, and suddenly
large expense will be incurred to give it
decent burial. Another coffin may be so worn
and rotten that the bones may be observed
protruding, and yet not the slightest effort
be made to repair or replace their receptacle ;
but let a curious foreigner be seen to take up
one of these bones in too inquisitive a manner,
and it may be the means of bringing down
upon him the vengeance of an entire village
of people.

Posthumous testimonials of a public nature
form a notable feature in Chinese streets and
highways. They consist of square frames of
stone, boasting little, if any, architectural

beauty, but often elaborately carved, and they may be seen spanning the main thoroughfares within a city, or lining the wayside at the suburban entrances outside the gates. The banks of the Grand Canal are abundantly studded with such monuments. They are, as a rule, testimonials to individual instances of official probity, filial piety, female purity, and conjugal fidelity, those representing the two last being considerably in the preponderance ; and they are erected either by the gentry of the district, or at their instance and that of the local executive by the Imperial command. The inscriptions upon them are generally limited to a record of the name of the individual, the special virtue it is desired to commemorate, and the date of the erection. Where the Emperor is the source of the honour conferred, one character, meaning "bestowed," is carved in a framework of dragons over the inscription. The case, described in a former chapter, of the self-sacrifice of an affianced girl, would probably earn for the heroine such a mark of public or even governmental approbation.

Mourning is of three kinds. There is the

three years' term, practically twenty-seven
months, which is worn for a parent or husband. Then the one year, worn for a grand-
parent, wife, brother, paternal uncle, &c.
And third, the five or three months, worn for
relations further removed on the male side.
Mourning is not worn for any female relative
other than mother, grandmother, or wife.
At funerals, especially of important kindred,
sackcloth is worn, but for permanent mourning white is the recognized colour. Where
it is very deep, the cap and shoes are white,
and white silk instead of black is entwined
amongst the plaits at the extremity of the
queue. The contrast in this custom to our
own is not so very startling, when it is remembered that so lately as three centuries
ago white was the mourning colour in England and some parts of Europe.

CHAPTER XV.

USE OF THE WRITTEN CHARACTER FOR DECORATION.

ANOTHER interesting fact connected with the Chinese, and one which has not received that attention from writers upon the country which it deserves, is the partiality shown by the people for their written character, and the extent to which it is applied for purposes of decoration. The taste exhibited in the advertisement by tradesmen of their business and wares has already been alluded to; yet the shop signs form but a small proportion of the inscriptions which attract the notice whilst traversing a Chinese city. Characters of all sizes and colours appear to teem in every direction and upon everything, until the careless traveller is apt to weary of the perpetually recurring hieroglyphic; but to the inquiring mind there is an interest in speculating what it all means, and the Chinese student will find in the collection a convenient opportunity for studying and acquiring a considerable proportion of the few thousand characters which should suffice to give him a practical knowledge of the language.

The wholesale manner in which some churches are decorated nowadays with texts, &c., will perhaps convey the nearest idea of the extent to which the character is used in the embellishment of public buildings and dwelling houses. Scarcely a wall, door, window, or pillar, but displays in some shape or another its scroll, tablet, or device, bearing some felicitous couplet, motto, or monogram, artistically inscribed. In the better class of houses the principal room is decorated with movable panelled doors, on each of which there is a spirited sketch with accompanying inscription in seal character or shorthand. The scrolls. mostly contain apophthegms or classical or poetical quotations, or they are inscribed with some impromptu sentiment, the autograph contribution of a distinguished person or friend ; where they are in pairs, antithesis in rhythm and signification are always

K

carefully studied, as, for instance, if we should write in English :

> The autumn breeze sighs through the pine trees,
> The summer zephyrs fructify the peach blossom.

Over the entrance to the door is generally written some sentence deprecatory of evil or imploratory of good. A not uncommon inscription is, " May the five blessings descend upon this door,"—the five being contentment, health, long life, wealth, success. Another common inscription is, " His Holiness Kiang is here; of nothing are we afraid." Kiang was a famous general of the Chow Dynasty who was peculiarly quick at discovering and exposing villainy of every kind, and was subsequently canonized in consequence. Panels of doors and windows are frequently decorated with the character "happiness." Another favourite word is "long life," and these two together, with a third, meaning "rich emolument," repeated in perpetually recurring series, constitute a favourite device for borderings and otherwise. Over shop doors of the humbler class may be seen the inscription, " Peace be to those who go out and come in;"

or again, "May wealthy customers perpetually arrive." On the opposite side of the street it is the custom to erect a blank wall or fence facing the door, so as to avert any evil influences from entering in. Upon this is generally pasted a slip of paper inscribed with the sentence : " Opposite to me may wealth arise ; " or : " On opening the door may I see good luck ; " or : " The Imperial beneficence is illimitable."

The temples teem with inscriptions, both in the shape of antithetical scrolls and ornamental tablets suspended horizontally. These are principally presented to the shrine by grateful or admiring votaries, and they have more or less reference to the attributes of the particular deity complimented. Those given to the temple to the tutelary divinity of Shanghae, situated in the tea-gardens there, will serve very well as specimens of the rest. Over the main entrance may be seen, " Universal joy for the people," and " Be there but a prayer, and the response must follow." The latter maxim possesses an interesting resemblance to our own Bible assurance, " Ask, and ye shall receive," &c., and it may

K 2

often be observed inscribed on little shrines upon the roadside in country places, showing the faith the people have in the efficacy of prayer. Further within the city temple may be observed several handsome slabs suspended over the principal halls. One is inscribed with the words, " Protection given to all people ; " a third, with " Power of protection unlimited ; " a fourth, with the precept, " All evil deeds avoid." It is considered a highly meritorious act to present a temple with a valuable inscription ; and, where the donor is a person of note or influence, care is taken to exhibit the gift in the most conspicuous position the temple has at disposal. In most temples a tablet may be seen placed in the most prominent position upon the principal altar, inscribed with the loyal prayer, " Long live the Emperor."

The rocks adjoining temples in romantic spots, which the Chinese, like all idolaters, are very partial to as localities for their shrines, are frequently covered with fantastic inscriptions in huge characters, deeply graven, so as to defy time and weather. Some of these are so ancient and so highly valued

that lengthy journeys are constantly under-
taken by antiquaries and others for the express purpose of obtaining rubbings, which
are afterwards handsomely mounted as scrolls,
and hung as we use pictures.

The large extent to which the character is
employed upon lanterns is a very noticeable
feature. A Chinaman and his lantern are
inseparable. Let him start on any errand
which is likely to occupy him until sunset,
and his lantern will be the first article that he
lays hands on to carry with him. Even on
the brightest moonlight night he considers it
his duty to provide himself with artificial
light; and it is a curious sight at a large fire
at night to see the crowds which fill the
streets, every man with his lantern held aloft,
although the very heavens are all ablaze with
light. This practice owes its rise, no doubt,
to the absence of any system of public light-
ing for the streets and highways. The lantern
has none the less its uses in daylight; suspended over doorways and along the fronts of
shops it declares the surname of the proprietor
within in huge characters, and no respectable
domicile is without one. Indeed all lanterns,

whether carried in the hand or otherwise, are
inscribed with the surnames of their owners,
so that whilst walking the street of a night a
man can always discern that his friend Jones
or Robinson is approaching, long before his
figure is discernible.   Official persons show
their titles on their lanterns, not their names,
a rule which is frequently abused by vaga-
bonds, who have only to show a lantern
inscribed with "The Magistrate" to be able
to extract money from the weak or unwary.
Wealthy families and officials affect the large
globular lantern, the common classes a smaller
one of cylindrical shape.   The characters are
always inscribed in red or black paint, save in
time of mourning, when blue is employed.
Lanterns form an important adjunct in all
processions, idolatrous, hymeneal, and funereal;
and on such occasions the larger the lantern
the more imposing is its effect considered.

The apparel of the Chinese again is constantly to be seen decorated with the written
character.   It is observable principally upon
the large cuff attached to the sleeves worn
by females and upon their little shoes, upon
children's caps and clothes, and upon the

snuff-bottles, tobacco-pouches, fan-cases, and girdle-ends of the men. The sketches on the fans used by both sexes are nearly always accompanied by inscriptions, and very often a specimen of caligraphy constitutes the sole ornament of the article, the highly-prized autograph of some relative, friend, or distinguished individual.

Numerous examples of the universal employment of the character in the decoration of articles for daily use may be seen in the cups, saucers, plates, chopsticks, teapots, vases, incense-burners, cabinets, and a hundred other things which find their way to this country as curiosities. Indeed, an entire book might be filled with illustrations of the various decorative purposes to which the Chinese character is put, and a vast store of additional facts as to the history, poetry, legendary lore, and customs of the Chinese might thus be elicited. Enough, however, has been advanced in this and preceding chapters to show how highly the Chinese prize their seemingly eccentric and impracticable symbols, but to them beautiful character, and that it is utilized by them to an extent unprecedented in the practice of any nation, ancient or modern; unless it be perhaps the Egyptians, to whose persistent habit of recording every phase of their social life in picture language upon their tombs, monuments, temples, and otherwise, we owe the wonderful insight into their manners and customs which indefatigable Egyptiologists have obtained for us.

CHAPTER XVI.

CHINESE PROPER NAMES.

NOTHING perhaps can sound more comical to the unaccustomed ear than the monotonous "ching, chong, chow, fee, fo, fum," of which sounds, with others like them, the Chinese syllabary appears principally to consist. Yet the Chinese symbols possess a wealth of meaning and expression of which few, if any, languages can boast; and in none perhaps are the proper names so universally composed of words which form part and parcel of the language itself. Consequently Chinese names, both of men and places, always have a meaning, and a large proportion of them are represented by words in common use.

Chinese surnames, which, as I have remarked in a former chapter, are but limited in number, are as a rule composed of but one character. Names are generally made up of two, and characters having a felicitous meaning are always selected. The surname always precedes the names. For example, supposing a man's name to be *Kung*, " Palace," and his names *Pao Yeng*, " Precious Recompense," his card would indicate him as *Kung Paoyeng*, "Palace Precious Recompense." Another man's surname may be *Wang*, " King," and his name *Ta Leuh*, " Great Six," probably from his being a sixth child or son. He would be styled *Wang Taleuh*.

In some provinces it is common amongst intimates to add the familiar prefix of *Ah* to the second character of the name : as, for example, the two persons just named would be severally called, *Ahyeng* and *Ahleuh*. And this will account for the numbers of *Ahfoos*, *Ahchows*, *Ahlums*, &c., to be met with amongst the natives of Canton. It is the usual practice with Chinese servants, especially those belonging to that province, when engaging themselves to foreigners, to give in merely their names with this familiar prefix, and many wealthy brokers and compradores in the trade are thus known and designated amongst foreigners. But the habit has its rise in the contempt which the Cantonese affect to have for foreigners, and it would not be tolerated

amongst themselves either between master and
servant or in business relations. Many and
many a time have I experienced the greatest
difficulty in inducing Chinese, who have come
before me to have agreements with British
subjects attested, to discover their proper surnames and names, there being such a rooted
aversion in their minds to commit themselves
by name to any arrangement entered into
with a foreigner.

Women's names are mostly selected from
amongst names of gems, flowers, virtues, and
such like, and are consequently quite in keep-
ing with the characteristics of the sex. On
marrying, a woman takes the surname of her
husband, as with us: but with the usual con-
trariety of the Chinese character, the affix
which marks the name of the married woman
is placed after the surname. The wife of Mr.
"Palace" would, for example, be designated
Kung She, or "Palace Madam."

Titles, official or otherwise, always precede
the name when stated in full. But when a
person is designated by his title familiarly
in conversation or writing, as, for instance,
where we should say Colonel A., or Commis-

sioner B., the Chinese place the title after the name.

Names of provinces, districts, cities, rivers, mountains, &c., derive their signification for the most part either from some characteristic of the locality or some legendary or family association connected with it. And it is seldom that any characters but those of a felicitous meaning are employed : *Quangtung* (anglicized into Canton) and *Quangsi* signify "broad east" and "broad west;" *Honan* means "south of the rivers;" *Hupeh*, "north of the lakes;" *Shantung*, "east of the hills;" *Hankow*, "mouth (or port) of the Han;" *Shanghae*, "ascending (or on) the sea;" *Pekin*, "northern capital;" *Nankin*, "southern capital;" *Newchwang*, "bullock farms;" *Foochow*, "happy district;" *Tientsin*, "celestial harbour;" *Amoy*, "summer gate;" *Chang Kea Khow*, "the gate of the Chang family;" *Tien Shan hu*, "lake of the celestial hills;" and so on.

The designations by which the various sorts of tea are known in the market may be worth notice, as coming under the more immediate observation of dwellers at home. Congo is a corruption of *Kungfu*, signifying labour,

and the Moning Congo advertised by tea-
dealers is simply a sort of the same tea grown
at *Wuning*, a district and city the name of
which, being interpreted, means "Military
Rest." Souchong signifies "little sprouts;"
Pekoe, "white down;" Bohea is derived from
the *Wuhee* Hills on which it is produced;
Oolung means "Black Dragon;" Hungmoey,
"Red Plum;" Campoi, "Selected firing;"
Hyson, "Fair Spring;" Twankay takes its
name from *Tunkee*, or "Beacon Brook;"
what is called "Young Hyson" is in Chinese
termed *Yutsëen*, or "Before the rains;"
Gunpowder the Chinese call *Yuen choo*, or
"Round Pearls." There are a number of
other names given to tea, but these will be
recognized as those most familiar to the European ear. What are termed "chop names"
are the fancy designations given by Chinese
dealers to their teas, after having been made
up into parcels of so many hundred chests
each. The tea is grown in the first instance
by small farmers, who carry the produce of
their respective gardens to the nearest depôt,
where it is collected by brokers, and by them
made up into chests for delivery to the dealers,

who convey it for sale to the foreign mart.
These dealers are very particular in the selection of high-sounding and felicitous titles for
their several parcels or chops, and very often
a particular chop acquires such a fame as to
be eagerly sought after for each successive
season.

CHAPTER XVII.

TRAVELLING AND PORTERAGE IN CHINA.

SCARCELY one Englishman in a thousand, doubtless, puts himself to the trouble of considering what means the Chinese have of travelling in their native country, or perhaps cares whether they move about at all. Yet it cannot but be an interesting question how so vast a territory is traversed by its teeming population, and in what way the merchandise of so active and commercial a people is conveyed to and fro. The true state of the case may be told in a few words. There is perhaps no spot on the face of the globe in which locomotion is so general and traffic so large, and yet where such clumsy and imperfect means of conveyance are provided, either for men or for goods.

Communication is carried on in China, as in most partially civilized countries, by means of roads and rivers or canals. But of roads, there is nothing at this moment that deserves the name. Traces are everywhere to be seen upon the great thoroughfares of the elaborately constructed highways of better days, but these are now mere broken tracks, obstructed throughout much of their course by the very stones which once constituted their source of utility and beauty. Bridges too, many of them admirable as works of art, and others curious from their rough and massive character, span wide and rapid streams, but like everything else in China, they tell the same sad story of past energy and present decay. With water communication, however, the country is extraordinarily well supplied, and although too many important channels show signs of having suffered from sheer neglect or wantonness, a vast network still exists which will certainly prove of immense service whenever a new life is instilled into the people by the introduction of foreign appliances and enterprise.

These highways and streams are always more or less alive with passengers and traffic proceeding from city to city. The conundrum, "Why are wheeled vehicles scarce in China?" with its reply, "Because there is only one Cochin-China," more nearly represents the fact

than the would-be-witty compiler at all intended, for no such thing as a carriage is
known in the country. In the northern provinces there is a sort of mule-waggon much
in vogue, composed of a square body clumsily
set on two wheels, and without the semblance
of a spring, even in the shafts, and which
the natives seem to think perfection; but the
tortures experienced by foreigners who have
been compelled to have recourse to them are
described as being most excruciating. In the
midland and southern provinces sedan-chairs
are mostly used. This is a vehicle very similar
to the ancient sedan of Europe, save that the
ends of the shafts, instead of being slung on
straps, are borne directly upon the shoulders,
and being made of bamboo or other elastic
material, they give an easy springing motion
to the conveyance. Where four bearers are
used, the shafts are slung to poles, one between
each couple of bearers before and behind, and
the motion becomes even more agreeable.
The pace, however, never exceeds a regular
three to four miles an hour. The use of
ponies, mules, and donkeys, is likewise universal, but it is seldom that an animal above

L

mediocrity in breed or condition is to be seen; and the vast majority are emaciated, over-worked creatures.

Tea and rest houses are to be found located everywhere, at easy stages from each other, many of them built or endowed by charitable individuals for the benefit of the wayfarer. Such establishments are sure to be met with on the tops of toilsome or dangerous mountain passes, not unfrequently with a small shrine attached, at which the traveller seldom omits to offer up incense or a prayer to propitiate the local deity into granting him a favourable journey.

Another favourite conveyance in China, is the wheelbarrow. Not anything like the vehicle known by that name amongst our-selves, but a more convenient and scientific-ally constructed affair. The wheel measures from three to four feet in diameter, and is so placed as to run under the centre of the body, which is a mere framework, with a ledge on either side, after the fashion of an Irish car. The passengers, for the machine will carry as many as four, sit on either side the frame with their legs outwards, or one or two will sit on the one ledge, balanced by their luggage on the other. The weight being thus poised upon the wheel as a centre, the barrow-man, who grasps a shaft in either hand, aided by a strap over the shoulders, has little to do beyond pushing and guiding the vehicle. The larger-sized barrows often have an extra man harnessed to the front to assist in tracking, and in the case of a long journey a tent of matting or cotton cloth is stretched over the top as a protection from the sun and rain, the opening lying backwards towards the driver. In some parts of China these barrow-men, when the wind happens to be strong and blowing in the right direction, convert it into a useful ally, by rigging out a couple of sprits, on which they hang a piece of sacking, or a patched coverlet, or an old jacket, or any other article of clothing which may come convenient, by way of a sail, the general effect being rather ludicrous, and scarcely worthy the poetical picture by which Milton has immortalized the practice. A curious incident connected with these same wheelbarrows, and indicative of the readiness with which the Chinese will forego their old-established usages, when it suits their purpose, occurred lately at Shanghae. Barrows were not in vogue at that port some fifteen years ago, their use being confined to a neighbouring district, and that only in limited numbers. Suddenly a demand for them arose with the growing traffic of the settlement, and they increased so rapidly within a brief space of time, that their numbers and excruciating noise became an intolerable nuisance, and stringent local ordinances had to be enacted to limit their complement to the necessities of the place, and to oblige their drivers to apply grease to the wheels and ply for hire only at particular stands.

The conveyance most frequently employed for travelling, however, is the boat, and it must be admitted that, setting aside the one element of speed, the Chinaman has carried his notions of locomotion by water to a high pitch of excellence. I refer of course only to inland communication. The varieties of craft employed in travelling are endless, from the tiny little cockle, like an egg-shell with one quarter cut out, to the huge two-storied barge, built to accommodate a Viceroy with all his belongings. Each variety of boat, moreover, is pertinaciously made to retain the stereotyped style of build which custom and the particular requirements of each district have assigned to it, and it is as easy to a Chinese to name the class of boat he needs, as it is for a Londoner wanting a cab to hail a Hansom or a four-wheeler. Boats cannot be engaged, however, as a rule, save through properly recognized registrars, appointed by the Government, and who are held responsible for the good behaviour of the boatmen whom they employ. In the majority of cases unhappily the arrangement results in both boatman and traveller becoming the subject of extortion, rather than in any better adjustment of the passenger traffic.

Passenger boats, and indeed most of the craft used in inland communication, are constructed of pine or other light material upon a framework of box, teak, or camphor. Every plank and rib is highly varnished, and the entire economy of partitions and divisions is so arranged as to be movable at pleasure. The roofs are water-tight, but movable nevertheless, and the sides are sufficiently supplied with windows of glass, gauze, or oyster-shell, for purposes of light and ventilation. In fact the interiors of the larger-class boats are furnished rooms in miniature, and they are wonderfully clean, convenient, and comfortable to travel in. The one drawback is their drafty character in winter weather, but in the summer they are excellent conveyances where time is no object. The method of propulsion chiefly relied on is the single scull, slung upon a pivot in the stern frame, and furnished with a broad long blade, which, being worked obliquely by a number of men from side to side in the water, drives the boat along nearly as effectually as does the European screw. When mandarins travel they select the largest and handsomest passenger boats that can be procured, and the moment the great man embarks a huge flag is hoisted, proclaiming his official rank, lanterns are perched upon the stern similarly inscribed, and the scarlet boards bearing his honorary titles, and conveying the commands to be silent, to stand back, &c., which are usually carried in procession before him, are displayed on either side of the boat in order to strike awe into persons passing by. When the individual is of unusually high rank, the local officials of each several district through which he passes are expected to greet him as he approaches their jurisdiction, to entertain him at their expense whilst passing through, and to escort him out again, each ceremony being accompanied by a loud banging of gongs and discharge of crackers. On leaving the passenger boat it appears to be the custom for the official traveller to bequeath his titular banner to the proprietor, for the sails and awnings of this class of boats are always made up of a patch-work of inscribed flags, as if to show the number of great men who have honoured them by their patronage.

The slow pace at which these passenger boats travel has necessitated the introduction of express or despatch boats, the fastest of which is undoubtedly the so-called "foot-boat" of Kiangsu, a sort of canoe capable of containing but one passenger, and propelled by a man sitting far back in the stern sheets, who works a pair of sculls with the soles of his naked feet, whilst his hands assist to steer with a paddle. These little craft push on day and night, successfully threading their

way through shallow channels or crowded
suburbs, where clumsier vessels could not
venture or move, and it is said that they can
easily do their seven miles an hour independently of wind or current.

Merchandise is even worse off than are
travellers for the means of safe and speedy
transit. Junks along the coast, and boats,
barrows, and carts inland, are the only conveyances at disposal besides human and animal
labour. In sea-going craft the Chinaman does
not shine, although there are few better
sailors in the world than are to be found
amongst the population of the seaboard provinces, and the courage and skill which they
exhibit in handling their clumsy crazy vessels
is something that needs to be seen to be believed. Their inland boats are very efficient
as far as convenience and carrying capacity
are concerned, and they are always most
ingeniously contrived to suit the exigencies
of the several streams in which they are
accustomed to ply; but they necessarily lack
the essential element of speed, a deficiency
which even the Chinaman is sufficiently alive
to his interest to regret, and endeavour all in

his feeble power to repair. There is, moreover, no system of insurance for inland craft,
and their flimsy construction, combined with
the numerous risks incident to river naviga-
tion, renders the transmission of goods by
them at all times more or less perilous.

The barrows of China have been already
described; they are used indiscriminately for
the conveyance of passengers and merchandise.
They are skilfully contrived to carry as much
weight as can possibly be trundled along
upon one wheel, but the largest of them is only
equal to a load of some seven hundred-weight,
and the labour which it must cost to push or
track this for miles, even along a level road,
must be enormous. But in order fully to
realize the gigantic toil to which a Chinese
will patiently subject himself and his animals,
as well as the indomitable perseverance which
he is capable of exhibiting in the face of
formidable obstacles, where trade is concerned,
the reader should for once see a cart-load of
heavy foreign bales being dragged up a de-
clivity upon a main thoroughfare in the north
of China. The cart is of the rudest construction possible, a mere raft of rough heavy

planks lying upon an axle of unhewn wood, and supplied with two wheels of solid timber. In the cruel clumsy shafts is a mule, starved and wretched to the last degree. Harnessed haphazard in front or alongside of it are two or three other sorry animals, whose race it were indeed hard to divine from their outward appearance. Sometimes a bullock or a man is put in to make up the team. The wheels of the machine stand jammed against a rough slab of granite placed ages ago as a stepping-stone, but now tilted up aslant, and only to be surmounted at the lower end. The driver of the cart utters an inhuman yell, cracks his thonged whip, and the unhappy beasts with a frantic rush and struggle manage to surmount the obstacle, only to be brought up again a yard or two farther in advance, when the same process has to be repeated, and so on over and over again at each successive step until the top is reached. The descent on the other side can be little less trying to the mule which has the ill-luck to occupy the shafts; and as for the goods, it is perhaps fortunate that they are only manufactures, and are well protected by strong canvas packing.

More might be added on the subject of
coolies, their capabilities, peculiar customs,
&c., but enough has been advanced to convey
a tolerably distinct idea of the manner in
which locomotion and carriage are accomplished in China, and to show, what after all
is my main object, how urgent a demand
there is, even in the interests of the Chinese
themselves, for the introduction of some of the
improvements in the conveyance of passengers
and goods which have rendered it so safe and
speedy a process in Western countries. That
the Chinese themselves possess sufficient intelligence to appreciate this want has already
been abundantly proved by the readiness with
which they charter and ship in foreign vessels,
both coastwise and on the rivers, and by the
continually increasing flow of passengers, who
prefer the security, certainty, and speed of
our steamers to the delay and loss incident to
the employ of their own craft. There can be
little doubt that when railways can once
obtain a foothold in the country, the Chinese
will be as quick to discern their vastly superior advantages as they have been to avail
themselves of our steamers and sailing ships.

CHAPTER XVIII.

THE CHARACTER OF THE CHINESE.

IT was observed in the introductory chapter
that the prevalent impression with regard to
the character of the Chinese people seems to
be that they have no notion of honour,
honesty, or courage, and that they are by
nature a cruel, merciless race. This estimate
is erroneous, and needs to be corrected. I do
not pretend to maintain that the Chinese are
free from the vices common to all humanity,
and I will even admit that they possess many
defects of character from which other peoples,
who have made even less progress than themselves, have been found to be exempt. At the
same time it is hardly fair to judge them by
that code which an advanced state of intelligence and civilization has taught us to set up
for our own guidance in respect to mental
and moral qualities, and straightway to
denounce them as weak or reprobate because
they cannot fulfil all the requirements of such

a standard. It must be remembered that they are at best but heathen, and that their advantages have been confined entirely to what the light of nature, and the teachings of sages long since ancient could afford ; and taking this circumstance into consideration, as well as the fact of their many ages of isolation, instead of there being any ground for special condemnation against them, there is, I conceive, much cause for marvel that they hold virtue and its kindred characteristics in such high estimation, and that their standard of what is good and commendable so nearly approaches that of more privileged and gifted nations.

The moral qualities of a people can only be judged of by such salient points in their character and conduct as come under the observation of those who study them, or are thrown into more or less intimate association with them ; and if this criterion be accepted as a just one, there is every reason for concluding that the Chinese are not so prone to evil and so dead to good as they have been made out to be. Their sense of honour, for example, although not of that

nature which is ready to resent the slightest
insult by pugnacious demonstration, is nevertheless very keen, and the educated classes
especially are painfully sensitive to insult or
indignity. This has been fully established by
the numerous instances which have occurred,
even within the limits of our brief acquaintance with the people, of public functionaries,
both high and low, who have sacrificed their
lives rather than desert their posts or sustain
disgrace. Cases have not been wanting moreover in mercantile experience, where traders
have been prepared to forfeit considerable
sums, or otherwise forego valued interests,
rather than belie their word, or permit their
own credit, or that of their connections to
suffer damage. The Chinese have not, it is
true, that delicate perception of what the claims
of truth and good faith demand which is so
highly esteemed amongst us Westerners, but
they know and prize both characteristics, and
practical illustrations thereof are constantly
observable in their relations one with another,
and with foreigners.   Although essentially a
commercial people, for example, they do not
appear to take such extraordinary precautions

against fraud in the course of business amongst themselves which are thought necessary with us. Written contracts do pass between man and man, but their use is frequently dispensed with, and they are never so formal in character as ours are. Even in intercourse with foreigners cases constantly happen where the Chinaman's honour is the sole guarantee to the merchant for the fulfilment of the agreement; and in the common course of foreign business, transactions of all magnitudes are usually closed by a simple entry in the foreigner's book, to which the Chinaman is supposed to attach his signature, although he cannot read a word of what is inscribed.

Honesty, moreover, is by no means a rare virtue with the Chinese. Witness the magnitude of the pecuniary interests which are at this moment confided by our merchants to compradores, servants, and friendly traders, and although instances have occurred in which this trust has been betrayed, more especially of late years, since the rapid extension of foreign commerce has induced a laxity in the choice of servants by merchants, yet they can safely be considered as altogether exceptional,

and attributable as much to the want of precaution on the one part, as to dishonesty on
the other. Look again at the security with
which merchants have often been able to commit large sums to native hands in the interior,
notwithstanding the tempting facilities given
to embezzlement by distance, inaccessibility,
and the known hesitation of the native authorities in detecting and punishing crime.
Against all this there is of course to be
quoted the large amount of litigation going
on at all the ports between foreigners and
Chinese in consequence of the failure of the
latter to fulfil their engagements ; but such
suits may also be fairly regarded as exceptional,
when considered in relation to the enormous
aggregate of the trade carried on between the
two peoples, and still more so when it is remembered that the majority of the litigants
on the erring side are petty traders or
brokers.

Nowhere perhaps is this tendency in the
main towards honesty more notable than
amongst the personal establishments maintained by foreigners at the ports. Their
houses are as a rule plentifully furnished with

articles of luxury and *vertu*, often of considerable value, very much as is the case with well-appointed residences in the West, and although the occupants never think of locking up even their jewellery, stray money, &c., yet it is rarely that anything is missed through the fault of the indoor servants. As far as my own experience of some thirty years' residence in the country is to be relied on, I can vouch for never having lost a single article save a small revolver, and that was restored a few days afterwards on my assembling the servants and appealing to their sense of right not to allow the stain of theft to rest on the household. They discovered the thief without difficulty, and he was soon obliged by the rest to leave my service. I am alluding of course to well-ordered establishments, where care is taken in the selection of servants. There are residents who do not take the precaution of being particular as to antecedents or character, and who are consequently perpetually being robbed, and unfortunately the outcry raised by such persons is apt to give a bad name to the entire servant class. I have also heard complaints made of peculation of liquors,

M

house stores, and such like. But then it is much less the habit in China to keep articles of this kind under lock and key than it is in England, and were similar latitude allowed in the latter country, the result I apprehend, if I may judge from what I have seen and heard of housekeepers' troubles at home, might prove quite as deplorable, if not even more so, than it is found to be in China. The pilfering of portions of merchandise in the course of transit between the ships and warehouses on shore has been also instanced as a proof of the dishonest tendencies of the Chinese; but when it is remembered how few and feeble are the precautions taken against theft in the matter of landing and shipping cargoes in China, as compared to the strict vigilance and scrutiny exercised under similar circumstances at home, and when moreover it is considered what crazy cargo boats are employed, and how much of the porterage to and fro is carried on by means of coolies, who proceed unaccompanied through crowded streets and by-lanes, it becomes rather a matter of surprise that the peculation is not far more extensive than it is.

Another practice to which the Chinese are very prone is that of wrecking, accompanied often by ill-treatment and even murder of the hapless mariners who fall into their hands. This is a crime which may be ascribed as much to want of enlightenment as to any natural propensity to dishonesty or cruelty; and the fact that, it is not so long since similar atrocities were common upon our own coasts, and amongst people who at any rate had been better taught, must present some ground of hope that the Chinese too may in time become reformed in this particular. It is not generally known moreover that it is the custom in China to regard waifs and strays as the rightful property of the finders, a primitive notion it is true, but one not to be wondered at in a country where might is still to a great extent right, and where the laws of salvage have yet to be framed. A Chinese would as soon think of asserting his title as of right to a lost property when found by another, as he would of appropriating that person's property as his own. I have seen large junks and timber rafts, which have broken away from their moorings in the Yangtsze river, coolly taken

M 2

possession of by parties of men and broken up
or divided, even although some of the proprietors might themselves be on board, and
the outrage would be quietly put up with by
the sufferers as a decree of fate. When the
British Consulate at Shanghae was burnt down
in 1870, there happened to be in my office about
1000*l.* worth of enamels, which the curiosity
dealers had sent there to be inspected by some
naval officers, who were likely to be purchasers,
and remembering these at the last moment
when the fire had got the better of the engines,
I ran some personal risk in my endeavours to
rescue the articles from the flames. The
following morning, when the owners made
their appearance, bemoaning their supposed
loss, they were as much astonished as my
servants were chagrined, at my delivering
the entire set back without charge or mulct of
any kind. And I heard afterwards that a
handsome present was sent to the latter in
consideration of the aid which they were
supposed to have given me in the removal of
the enamels out of the burning house. The
above instances will show what the native
notion is in respect to salvage, but there is no

reason why it should not yield to better teaching and more stringent laws. Much may be effected too in the way of prevention and reform on the sea coast, both by foreign men-of-war and the foreign-built cruisers which the Chinese are now building. And it would always be wise in foreign governments to mark the few instances of kindly treatment of shipwrecked men which do at times occur by liberal rewards to all concerned.

As regards the question of courage, again it must be admitted that the Chinese possess more of the quality than they have hitherto had credit for. In almost every engagement between our men and theirs during the time that we were at war with them, instances were observed of really valorous conduct both in individuals and bodies of men, and the opinion was often expressed by those competent to judge, that had their armies and fleets been better found, armed, and officered, our successes might have been somewhat less easily won. This was clearly exemplified by the coolness with which the transport or "coolie corps," attached to our army in the Pekin campaign, was found to

go into action in the face of galling fires, as
well as by the steadiness and courage evinced
by the Chinese troops during the rebel campaign under Colonel Gordon and his staff of
foreign officers.

One element of courage, namely, careless-
ness of life or limb in the pursuit of an object,
is undoubtedly a Chinese characteristic. During
the occupations by our troops of Ningpo and
Chusan, instances repeatedly occurred of
Chinese ignoring the challenge of a loaded
sentry, and even braving bayonet or bullet for
some ridiculously trivial purpose, such as pursuing a long accustomed path, or pilfering
some small article hardly worth the trouble
of carrying off.   I myself was witness to
temerity of this kind when stationed as inter-
preter with a small detachment of troops at
Chinhai in 1842.   We were perched up in a
castellated joss-house on an isolated hill near
the coast about three to four hundred feet
high, and being in the midst of the enemy
and entirely removed for the time being from
all chance of succour, we were compelled to
draw a line round the foot of the hill, and to
give notice that every one who ventured

within the limits should be shot. Notwithstanding this threat and · our presumed
readiness to put it into execution, fishermen
would come daily at low ,water to pick up
shell-fish on the beach, and would coolly per-
sist in continuing the operation in spite of
" thud " after " thud " of the sentries' bullets
in the mud alongside of them, until at last,
for mere humanity's sake, they had to be left
alone. A small brig of war that was block-
ading the mouth of the river close by had the
same trouble with the trading and fishing
boats. The crews of these deliberately per-
sisted in trying to push in or out, notwithstanding the round shot that would crash
past their junks and at times sink one or two
of their number. I have observed a similar
indifference to peril at Foochow when the
river is flooded, and its stream of some thousand yards in width rushes madly through
the ancient and rough but sturdy stone bridge
which connects the two suburbs. Fragments
of timber rafts and debris of all kinds will
then get tangled together so as to block the
narrow arches near the centre, and natives
will fearlessly leap on to the heaving mass,

and, detaching a large piece of timber here
or there, will rush with it clasped in their
arms down through the surging torrent under
the bridge, in the hope of coming up safe at
the other side, and being able to make a few
coppers by the sale of their booty. I have
seen many accomplish the feat successfully,
but I was informed that cases of drowning
were by no means unusual.

It will be more difficult perhaps to defend
the Chinese from the charge of being cruel.
That they lack that sensitiveness which cannot tolerate the idea of causing unnecessary
pain, is undoubtedly proved by the inhuman
character of their legal penalties, by the
barbarous manner in which they treat their
prisoners, by the heedlessness with which
they will contemplate the infliction of torture
or of death in its most revolting forms, and
even by the merciless method in which they
carry their pigs, fowls, and other live stock
to market. Yet it cannot be rightly asserted
that the Chinese are naturally of a blood-
thirsty disposition. They are of too mild,
gentle, and forbearing a nature to admit of
the charge being strictly applicable. They

shrink with horror from the needless deprival of animal life, a notion perhaps Budhistic in its origin, but none the less common to all the sects of the people; and the mere sight of a cut finger or broken nose will occasion more bemoaning and fuss than a fractured limb or a ghastly wound would beget amongst Europeans. On the other hand this native gentleness and timidity disappear when horrors present themselves wholesale before the Chinaman's mind. Although he will rouse the neighbourhood if a little blood is drawn by accident or in a petty quarrel, yet he will munch his rice unconcernedly whilst human victims are undergoing torture or decapitation by the score in the next street.

The truth is that both kindliness and cruelty, gentleness and ferocity, have each its place in the Chinese character, and the sway which either emotion has upon their minds depends very much upon the associations by which they are for the moment surrounded. When in their own quiet homes, pursuing undisturbed the avocations to which they have been accustomed, there are no more harmless, well-intentioned, and orderly people. They actually appear to maintain order as if by common consent, independent of all surveillance or inter-ference on the part of the executive. But let them be brought into contact with bloodshed and rapine, or let them be roused by oppression or fanaticism, and all that is evil in their dispositions will at once assert itself, inciting them to the most fiendish and atrocious acts of which human nature has been found capable. It is not impossible that they owe much of this tendency to the extreme rigour of their code, and to the cruelty as well as frequency with which they see its penalties carried into effect, as also to the vast amount of want and woe to which their minds become habituated in the ever-recurring series of famines and rebellions that devastate the country. Could their laws, which, although rigorous, are after all well suited to the genius of the people, but be more justly and humanely administered, and could national disaster be rendered less frequent or terrible in its effects by the exercise of a wiser and more vigorous policy on the part of the government, there is every reason to believe that the better tendencies of the people would soon gather strength, and that the more ferocious part of their nature would in time be tempered into a true and manly courage.

But the phases of character in which the Chinese possess the most interest for us Western peoples are those which so peculiarly fit them for competing in the great labour market of the world. They are good agriculturists, mechanics, labourers, and sailors, and they possess all the intelligence, delicacy of touch, and unwearying patience which are necessary to render them first-rate machinists and manufacturers. They are, moreover, docile, sober, thrifty, industrious, self-denying, enduring, and peace-loving to a degree. They are equal to any climate, be it hot or frigid; all that is needed is teaching and guiding, combined with capital and enterprise, to convert them into the most efficient workmen to be found on the face of the earth. In support of these assertions it is only necessary to refer to our experience of them in America, Australia, India, and the Eastern Archipelago. Wherever the tide of Chinese emigration has set in there they have proved themselves veritable working bees, and made good their footing to the exclusion of less quiet, less exacting, less active, or less intelligent artizans and labourers. Even in China they have already proved their worth by helping to construct, under foreign super-intendence, men-of-war of first-class workman-ship and formidable proportions; and their artificers are daily acquiring increased skill in the arsenals now in active work at Tientsin, Shanghae, and Foochow. The marvellous energy of which they are capable as mere labourers is moreover constantly exhibited at the port of Shanghae, where they have been known to accomplish the discharge of a ship in less time, as I have been assured, than can be effected by dock-labourers at home, even with all the appliances of cranes and otherwise which these latter have at disposal.

This remarkable aptitude shown by the Chinese for skilled as well as physical labour is worthy the serious attention of both em-ployers and workmen in these days of strikes in every department of British skill and industry. If the Chinaman can thus compete with our artizans and working men in his native country, notwithstanding the many disadvantages which must attend the exercise there of his intelligence and strength, what will he not be able to accomplish when encouraged and taught to rival a foreign antagonist on his own ground, and at a more moderate rate of remuneration than the latter can afford to demand? Should matters go on as they are now doing in England, the labouring and manufacturing classes must not wonder if they find themselves ere very long displaced and distanced by the hitherto despised, but none the less practical, useful, and labour-loving Chinaman.

CHAPTER XIX.

CONCLUDING REMARKS.

IT will be seen from the foregoing chapters
how foreigners are situated in China, what
position they hold relatively to the people
amongst whom they dwell, and what characteristics of the latter come more prominently
under their observation. It remains now to
state the result of the intercommunication,
thus far, between the two races, foreign and
Chinese, and to hazard a few conjectures as to
what may be looked for in the future.

Two persons cannot be thrown into each
other's company for any considerable period
without an influence of some kind being exercised by the one upon the other, either for good
or for evil. With nationalities the same rule
holds good, and it is well worth considering
what has been the influence in this instance,
and in which direction. As the stronger
more pushing, and more self-asserting people,

foreigners, it might be taken for granted, would be able to show the preponderance of influence to have been on their side, and such has been the case no doubt in a commercial and political point of view. A trade has been exacted, which has developed itself, in spite of obstructions of a vexatious and persistent character, into vast dimensions, and China has been compelled to take up a definite position, relatively to other nations, whether she likes it or no. But the amount of good concomitantly effected is questionable. The Chinaman's favourite motto, that "commercial intercourse enriches nations," has certainly received practical illustration in the material enrichment of various towns and districts more immediately connected with the foreign trade. But it may be doubted whether this good has not been more than counterbalanced, in the one case, by the immeasurable misery which has been occasioned by the rebellions, indirectly brought about (as has been demonstrated) by repeated collisions with Western powers, and, in the other case, by the introduction of opium, the sad effects of which have hitherto been ever on the increase.

There are the beneficial results of missionary teaching to be brought into account, but these, it has been shown, are so far infinitesimal as compared to the bulk of the nation, and even they too would fail, I fear, to bring the preponderance on the right side. As for any moral influence that foreigners may exercise by their mere presence in the country, it may be regarded as simply *nil.* Could a few fires be kindled here and there on the edge of an iceberg, the results, in dissolving those portions of the frozen mass immediately in contact with the flames might be greater, comparatively speaking, than the transforming effects which have as yet transpired through the presence of the few handfuls of foreigners scattered amongst the millions of the Chinese. Indeed, if anything, the influence has tended the other way, for I have found as a rule that Chinese do not improve by being brought into intimacy with foreigners, and by adoption, as a consequence, of their habits and ideas. The few Europeanized Chinese that are to be met with are, with very rare exceptions, most insufferable creatures.

The people generally of course know us

better than they once did, and the inhabitants
of those districts which have been most resorted
to by us would, I think, for the most part be
glad to increase this acquaintance, not only
on grounds of self-interest, but from their own
natural kindly feeling. But the ruling and
influential classes still only tolerate our
presence in the country, and I firmly believe
they would hail the day when they could see
(were such a thing possible) the last foreign
factory razed to the ground, and the last ship
dismissed the coast, *malgré* the loss to the
national revenue, and the ruin of the districts
dependent on our trade that would certainly
ensue. Experience of our more advanced
civilization and our improved appliances
appears to have taught the Chinese no permanent lesson as yet. Returning emigrants
fall back instinctively into their native notions
and conceits, looking back upon their foreign
sojourn as an ordeal happily over. Even men
of some pretence to social position, who have
of late years visited the West in a quasi-diplo-
matic capacity, have shown no sign of having
been impressed by what they have observed,
or moved to introduce like innovations and

N

advantages into their own country. Chung
How, the only really high-class mandarin who
has visited Europe, disappointed me keenly
when I was conversing with him last August,
by exhibiting the most listless indifference
to my suggestions as to the vast collection of
novel and interesting sights which it would
be well for him to see whilst in this country.
I happened to attend him at Shanghae when
he embarked for the first time on board of one
of the finest vessels of the French Messageries
fleet, and took possession of his cabin for the
voyage.   The next time when I met him was
in his handsome room at the Grosvenor Hotel
a day or two after his arrival.   Yet on both
occasions he took as little heed of his novel
surroundings as he would have done when
stepping on board of one of his own wretched
Chinese junks or walking into one of his still
more primitive native hotels.   To my mind
there must be something more in this than
an affected indifference arising out of simple
conceit.   It must be the result of an inborn
incapacity in the untutored Chinese mind to
entertain any subject save by the particular
process of thought, or in connection with the

particular association to which it has been schooled by custom and tradition.

To all this it may be replied that our foreign steamers and ships have been largely availed of by the Chinese, more especially of late years, both for passage and conveyance of merchandise; and that at various points upon the coast the Government has instituted arsenals upon a considerable scale under foreign superintendence, and capable of turning out formidable men-of-war, constructed upon the newest models, as well as arms and ammunition upon the most novel and destructive principles. This is so far true; but as regards Chinese passengers and shippers in foreign vessels, I have repeatedly mixed with and conversed with them when travelling in their company, and I have never observed the betrayal of a single emotion of admiration or wonder at the amount of science, labour, or means expended in the construction of the very vessels in which they or their goods were being conveyed, although most of these now plying on the Yangtsze river are specimens of some of the largest and finest river steamers that the Americans can build. On

the contrary, I have heard the terms " bar-
barian " and " foreign devil " freely employed
at such times by Chinese conversing amongst
themselves.   And I verily believe that most
of these travellers in first-class foreign vessels
have in every case returned to their several
homes only to ridicule or sneer at the out-
landish people amongst whom they have for
the moment been thrown ; although fully
appreciating doubtless, all the while, the
comfort and rapidity with which they have
been carried, and the security and dispatch
attending the transit of their merchandise.
The establishment of large and effective
arsenals by the Government loses much of
its value as an indication of influence in
favour of progress, from the fact, as I believe,
that the innovation has been adopted with the
object of so improving the offensive appliances
of the country as to place it in a position to
cope with foreign powers, when a favourable
opportunity offers for realizing that dream of
eventual ejectment, which still lingers in the
brain of the majority of Chinese statesmen.

There have been those who have asserted,
from high places and in authoritative style,

that the Chinese desire progress, and many
English and American newspapers have echoed
the sentiment.   But it is a mistake; and
those who initiated the cry too readily allowed
their eyes to be blinded to the fact that it was
a mistake.   One has only to live amongst the
people, to correspond and converse with the
mandarins, and to study the numerous memorials addressed to the throne by leading statesmen, to convince oneself, that, however much
portions of the trading section of the population would like to see foreign relations extended,
the ruling powers deprecate progress for its
own sake even at the slowest rate of advance,
whilst the mass of the people are altogether
indifferent to the subject.   And that such
should be the case need not be a matter of
surprise.   Progress to the Chinese mind represents the free introduction into the country
of a pushing, self-willed, impracticable, and
eccentric race, whose notions and habits are
utterly at variance with anything to which
they have hitherto been accustomed.   The
honest and patriotic mandarin can only discern in progress political complication, social
revolution, and perhaps general rebellion;

whilst the unscrupulous official foresees in it
an inevitable end to the monopolies and extor-
tions which he has been accustomed to regard
as legitimate sources of profit. The priest-
hood and literati can only discover in progress
an aggressive influence before which time-
honoured institutions, superstitions, and usages
must in time give way. The mechanic, agri-
culturist, and carrier contemplate progress
with an indefinite fear that it cannot co-exist
with the means of livelihood on which they
and their fathers have depended for generations. The merchant and shopman alone may
foresee in progress a possible source of advantage in the increasing profits which an extension of trade may bring about, but so small a
proportion of these latter classes is as yet in
a position to experience the practical results
of an extended intercourse, and they are so
tied down by their conservative instincts and
by their associations with the other classes of
society, that they are not equal to even the
feeblest protest against the universal prejudice.
Added to all this, the general experience of
intercourse with foreigners thus far has not
been such as to encourage the opposite way

of thinking. Under these circumstances who can blame the Chinese for preferring to remain as they are, as far as it is possible to do so, and deprecating any innovation upon the groove in which, as they imagine, they have moved so happily and successfully for thousands of years past?

But it by no means follows that progress is to be despaired of in the future of China. Further shocks and awakenings through collisions with foreign powers must occur, for the Chinese government is as yet too much wrapped up in notions of its strength and self-importance to appreciate the expediency of framing its policy so as to suit the times, and it cannot go on shilly-shallying indefinitely, one moment solemnly accepting international obligations, and another moment covertly receding from them. And whenever such collisions take place, they must inevitably be followed by the forcible introduction of new ideas, to the disruption of old-established and cherished usages. We can only hope that when the shock does come, the aggressive influence may be wielded by a wise and humane power, and that it may be so directed as to accomplish what is needed for the country with the least possible amount of loss and calamity to its unhappy people. At the same time I am not one of those who advocate an abrupt and unreasoning obtrusion of progress, as we understand the term, upon the country, either by force or persuasion. China is by no means ripe for an instantaneous reception throughout her entire territory of the highly advanced condition of civilization to which we and other Western peoples have become accustomed. There is abundant material to work upon, and that of the most plastic character : only it needs to be approached with caution, and worked with discretion ; otherwise there is a risk of exciting suspicion, explosion will follow, and the cause of progress will be thrown back for years.

There is no more intelligent and manageable creature than the Chinaman, so long as he is treated with justice and firmness, and his prejudices are to a reasonable extent humoured. He is distinguished moreover, like ourselves, by strong commercial instincts, which he will follow out even to the sacrifice of his native obstructiveness, conservatism, and conceit. The experience of the past thirty years has shown how readily Chinese traders will fall in with commercial ventures promoted or maintained by foreign capitalists, and it is easy to foresee how, in the openings that are now every day offering at the ports for the initiation of new enterprises, our merchants will find abundant opportunities for turning this love for trade to good purpose, by the introduction step by step of railways, steamers, and telegraphs, those three great feeders of commerce and pioneers of progress. Their love of literature, already alluded to, is another weak point in their armour of obstructiveness, against which efforts in the direction of progress may be usefully directed. Books on popular subjects, and newspapers or other periodical publications, provided the style is pure and classical, will always be read with avidity, and cannot fail to exercise a most beneficial effect in dispelling prejudice and error. Missionaries, as I have said, have already done something in this direction, but if they could be induced to give more pains towards suiting the style of their tracts to the attainments of the educated classes, and to confine themselves less to strictly religious subjects, and if our lay linguists could be persuaded to employ more of their spare time in Chinese composition, their united efforts would go far towards promoting a progressive tendency.

But the ameliorating effects of an extending trade and increasing knowledge, must ever be seriously neutralized unless the Chinese Government and people are also rightly affected by the policy which is pursued towards them by the several foreign governments with which they have international relations. This must be firm and uncompromising in the maintenance of treaty stipulations, and the exaction of every right which foreigners resorting to the country are reasonably entitled to. No shifts and excuses of any kind should be admitted. The interests of all foreign nations in this particular are identical. The laxity hitherto permitted in the matter of a personal audience of the Emperor, is one of the concessions which have occasioned material prejudice to foreign interests in China, and until the demeaning position in which Western powers are placed thereby is put an end to, they cannot hope to secure for their respective nationals that consideration with the officials and people generally, which is alone compatible with relations of a friendly and confiding nature. Every coolie in the empire is astute enough to discern that so long as his emperor and high mandarins do not consider foreigners worthy of being met and entertained on equal terms, there is no call for him to treat them with civility. It is a mere evasion for the Chinese to plead that Prince Kung and other high functionaries of Peking receive and call upon the foreign representatives, and so practically carry out the spirit of the treaty. It is a compromise which is tolerated it is true, but failing access to the fountain head, it is as demeaning to the recipients in the eye of the natives, as would be considered amongst us the vicarious reception and entertainment of a guest through a retainer or head-servant in the house. If an excuse has been offered on the ground of the minority of the Emperor, it is more than probably a blind, put forward to delay the evil day. Unless I am much mistaken, there is no honest intention to modify the existing position when the majority does occur, and it will not be done eventually unless the whole of the treaty representatives take a combined and determined stand against any continuance of the indignity, or unless some one of them is in a position to threaten coercive measures.

A writer in a late Hong Kong paper has very pertinently remarked, that although the solution of the audience question in a direction favourable to foreign views implies a violent wrench to every tradition surrounding an ancient and illustrious throne, and that consequently every sympathy is due to those whose patriotic instincts will suffer thereby, yet it cannot be admitted that the mass of Chinese officials have any claim upon foreign consideration in the matter. The ill government of many a cycle, which is mainly attributable to the difficulty hitherto existing in bringing matters to the immediate cognizance of the emperors without the intervention of interested officials, would alone justify intervention in favour of a change; but apart from this consideration, foreign interests in the country have now reached that magnitude that they imperatively demand that the existing isolation of the Emperor should be done away with at the very earliest opportunity.

Another essential measure necessary to progress, and which has not had that attention that it deserves, is the giving of official publicity to every act of concession to a foreign power. The treaties have not been promulgated and made law throughout the empire as they ought to have been, although in some of them publication to the people constitutes one of the provisions stipulated for ; and the consequence is that mandarins in the provinces constantly profess ignorance of the existence of trading privileges, and the inhabitants need not necessarily be aware of them. Even the concession of the non-audience claims will fail of effect, unless the fact that the Emperor has admitted a foreign representative to his presence be proclaimed by Imperial edict, and an injunction conveyed that all foreigners are to be treated accordingly. Officials and people alike will then see that their Government is in earnest in admitting foreigners to friendly relations on terms of entire equality, and will readily do their part in making friendly advances.

To recapitulate. Let the commercial enterprise of the people be taken advantage of
to introduce the thin end of the wedge of
progress wherever and whenever the opportunity offers itself; let knowledge be sown
broad-cast throughout the land by means of
suitable and instructive publications in the
native language ; and let foreign powers combine to treat China justly, and at the same
time see to it that she acts as justly by them,
and not only will progress be possible, but no
long time need elapse before a regeneration
ensues, which shall at once satisfy the longings
of the diplomatist, the merchant, and the
missionary.

APPENDIX.

THE selection of Chinese music is exceedingly limited, and what little there is can scarcely be said to vary much in its character. The accompanying is a ditty supposed to be sung by a Chinese beggar, and it will very well serve as a specimen of their few songs. A literal translation of the words is appended ; it would have been versified but that it proved impossible to retain the sense entire, and yet suit the number of syllables to the bars. The air was originally noted down by the Rev. E. Syle, of Shanghae. To render the song in the true Chinese style, it must be sung as much as possible through the nose.

Shuoh Fung Yang, Huah Fung Yang, Fung Yang Yuan sheko

Haou te fang, Tsze tsung chuh liaou, Chu Huang te,

Shi nien tao yew, Kew nien huang. San nien shuy ta,

san nien han, San nien huang chung, Kiang tsae yang.

Ta hoo jin kia, mai tien te, Siaou hoo jin kia,

mai ur lang; Wo kia mur yew, ur lang mai,

rall. . . . .

Pay liaou hua koo, shang kiai fang. . . .

Fungyang says one; *Fungyang* cries another; *Fungyang* always
was a nice place:

Ever since the days of Emperor *Chu;* its fields have been waste
nine years out of ten:

For three years it pours; for three everything is dried up; and
for the other three locusts bring distress:

Rich people sell their lands; poor people part with their little
ones:

I, alas! have no little ones to sell; so I shoulder my tambourine
and parade the streets.

For EU product safety concerns, contact us at Calle de José Abascal, 56–1°,
28003 Madrid, Spain or eugpsr@cambridge.org.

www.ingramcontent.com/pod-product-compliance
Ingram Content Group UK Ltd.
Pitfield, Milton Keynes, MK11 3LW, UK
UKHW012346130625
459647UK00009B/567